HEAVEN

*Who's Got
the Tickets
&
How Much
Do They Cost?*

MARTHA BOSHART

BARBOUR
PUBLISHING, INC.
Uhrichsville, Ohio

Mr. and Mrs. Elton Moser
R.R. 1 Box 204A
Copenhagen, NY 13626-9761

HEAVEN

Who's Got the Tickets

& How Much Do They Cost?

© 2001 by Martha Boshart.

ISBN 1-58660-239-X

All rights reserved. No part of this publication may be reproduced or transmitted in any form or by any means without written permission of the publisher.

All Scripture quotations are taken from the King James Version of the Bible.

Published by Barbour Publishing, Inc., P.O. Box 719, Uhrichsville, Ohio 44683 http://www.barbourbooks.com

Member of the
Evangelical Christian
Publishers Association

Printed in the United States of America.

DEDICATION

*In loving memory of
two of the greatest parents God ever created—
my parents, Lloyd and Naomi Boshart.*

CONTENTS

ACKNOWLEDGMENTS

Most of the stories in this book involve people I know. Without those people and without their part in the stories, I would not have been able to write this book. Together, they have enriched my life, warmed my soul, and put a heartbeat into what would otherwise be just words. To all of you who recognize yourselves in these pages, I sincerely thank you. I especially want to thank those of you who may feel some personal pain as these pages serve as a mirror, forcing you to relive difficult moments and events. I pray that the discomfort you may feel in reliving these stories will be tempered by knowing someone else has been blessed by reading them.

About halfway through this book project, I became hopelessly bogged down and discouraged. I am deeply indebted to one man for bailing me out—Norman Rohrer of Christian Writers' Guild. Several years ago I took his writing course and though I never completed it, he never gave up on me. Without his mentoring and encouragement, I would not have had the heart to go on.

My sister, Mary Honer, is a recently retired English teacher. Long before she retired, she began reading and editing this book, chapter by chapter. She has given many sleepless nights and endured many sleepy days to help polish these pages. To her, a very special "thank you."

Another sister, Cathy Roshan Khan and the one with whom I live, is a native of Pakistan, and English is her second language. She read and reread every chapter for clarity and gave many helpful suggestions for sharpening the meaning of some of my more muddied thoughts. To her also, a very special "thank you."

Two other people agreed to review this manuscript. They are Audrey Dorsch and Carrie M. Wood, both fellow members of Christian Writers' Fellowship International (CWFI). Their insights and suggestions have been invaluable in this final version. In addition, every member of CWFI has stood faithfully with me, cheering me on, even in those times when there appeared to be little to cheer about. "Thank you" is hardly a sufficient tribute for all they have taught me enroute to this book.

The rest of my family, along with a very wide circle of friends, have surrounded me with their enthusiasm, and let me tap from their stamina when my own supplies of both were depleted. I would not have survived in this endeavor without them.

INTRODUCTION

In thirty years of counseling I have talked with, hurt with, cried with so many people who find talking difficult, don't want to hurt, try not to cry, and either don't enjoy or have little time to read. This book is for all of them. It is intended to put into one readable source a blueprint for getting on the only road to heaven—and then putting some inspiration into the trip.

Bon voyage!

MARTHA M. BOSHART

1

THE TICKET

The name of Jesus Christ of Nazareth,
whom ye crucified,
whom God raised from the dead. . .
Neither is there salvation in any other;
for there is none other name under heaven
given among men, whereby we must be saved.

ACTS 4:10, 12

Several years ago I bought what is commonly called a
"boombox." The salesman requested that I also buy a
full-warranty policy to augment the limited warranty
supplied by the manufacturer. I was a bit annoyed,
thinking, *How totally insured must one be?*

Not long after the limited warranty expired, I found out. I marched back to that store with my now malfunctioning boombox and demanded just compensation. The saleslady's response was polite and gentle, but it thundered in my ears. "Did you buy the full warranty when you bought the box?"

Heavens! I thought. *She must be kidding.*

I was a frequent customer in this renowned store and I felt that I, and their merchandise, deserved a higher level of consideration. I relentlessly pursued the theme until that dear saleslady began looking almost convinced—not that I was right, but that I might become ruthless in my persistence.

She called the manager. I braced myself for more combat as this imposing hulk of a man, decades my junior, approached me. I will never forget what happened next. In a gesture of totally unexpected and unmerited clemency, he addressed me by name and said, "I'm going to honor that full warranty as if you had bought it. I'll give you a new boombox free of charge."

I walked out of there with much more than a new piece of merchandise in my hand. That young gentleman had reminded me, in one humbling spectacle, of the undeserving grace of God by which I will one day walk out of this world, and, although totally unworthy, enter heaven with a brand-new body, free of charge, because one man bought the full warranty with His life.

How Can Anybody "Choose" to Miss Heaven?

Incredibly, many people are going to miss heaven. I wish that were not true, but there are only two roads on which to travel through life. One leads to hell and the other to heaven.

Whether we like it or not, we have all taken a bite out of that forbidden apple in the Garden of Eden. That simple but profoundly disobedient act back there transformed two sinless human beings and every single human being thereafter into (brace yourself!) sinners. From then on, human nature at its core has been hopelessly corrupt, and a lifetime of benevolence and sacrifice will not effect a cure.

There is something inherently troublesome about all that. If this were a conversation rather than a book, we might be in a spirited dialogue by now. The idea of being born a sinner smacks of a genetic deformity requiring a physician. The notion that there are only two roads on which to travel through life seems unnecessarily limiting and might tempt one to consult a different map. And the mere mention of hell as an unsolicited final destination could easily pass as a cruel hoax or a loathsome joke.

The fact is, however, we really *are* born needing a physician, and life's atlas really does contain only one road map, and hell really is a cruel, loathsome, awful place. The significance of this single set of facts is so critical that if one messes up on even one of them, the whole set is faulty. That is the bad news.

There Is Good News!

But there is good news. The great physician can heal our genetic deformity. The atlas maps out *another* road, and narrow as it is, it leads to a destination so utterly unlike hell, one wonders why anyone would risk missing it. In fact, that destination is downright heavenly.

In a few days, I'm going on a vacation to a part

of the country where meteorologists tease the world almost daily with reports of sunshine and warm temperatures. I live in the East where I've sat in an abominable snowbank all winter. Easter has come and gone, and I'm still sitting in a snowbank. As you might imagine, sunshine and warm temperatures sound heavenly. But contrary to one of the most misleading of popular myths, earth has no hell to match the relentless, tormenting agony of the real place and no heaven worthy of comparison to the bliss and grandeur of the real Paradise.

Exactly What Is the Ticket?

How do we get to heaven, that is the question. Hell is easy; you simply do nothing but follow your own natural and selfish inclinations. Ironically, you can work yourself silly engaging in every conceivable good deed and donating to every charitable project, and that won't get you to heaven either. If good deeds and noble generosity were the ticket, can you imagine the frenzied competition for admission and the lobbying for rank?

The poor fellow crucified next to Jesus at Calvary wouldn't have had a gambler's chance at heaven if admission were contingent upon doing good. He was a criminal. His crucifixion was deserved. He was limping the last lap to defeat and hell. But something happened there at Calvary that dramatically and miraculously changed the outcome. The thief, first of all, admitted he was guilty. Then he acknowledged that Jesus was not. Finally, he addressed Jesus as Lord, a truly humble recognition that this man next to him was no ordinary person. He was the Savior, and the thief knew he needed a Savior really fast.

That was all it took. At that instant, Jesus declared the thief as eligible for Paradise as if he had never been a felon. It sounds too good and too easy to be true. Ordinarily, if something sounds too good to be true, it probably is. But this was no ordinary event. It never is ordinary when a person bound for hell takes that humble trek to Calvary and exchanges death for life.

Most people have little problem admitting Jesus was real and that He was an extraordinary person and even that He got himself crucified. Crucifixions were common two thousand years ago, and many who think about the matter at all assume Jesus was simply not crafty or savvy enough to talk His way out of the clutches of His accusers. Some even think He actually was guilty and deserved to die. What they don't realize is that "The cross did not *happen* to Jesus; He came on *purpose* for it" (Oswald Chambers). In fact, He had the divine audacity to say that His dying on that cross paved the one and only way to get to heaven.

How in the world did that thief at Calvary figure that out so quickly, just in time to die right? Most of us have a whole lifetime to figure it out, and many still don't get it straight. What a tragedy!

Think for a moment about the amount of time you spend ensuring that you make the best possible decisions about the food you eat, the clothes you wear, the TV programs your children may watch, the people upon whom you bestow the honor of your friendship, the political candidates you will support, your monetary investments. . . . I could go on and on. You may not attend to each of these issues every day, but, chances are, at least some of them daily occupy your prime-time peak efficiency moments. You take decision-making seriously.

Getting on the road to heaven is also a decision.

Have you ever considered that? You can't buy it or earn it or inherit it. You certainly, however, can miss it. Incidentally, there was a second malefactor hanging on a cross at Calvary. Unlike the first thief, this one denied his guilt, mocked and taunted Jesus, and stubbornly ignored the pleadings of his criminal colleague to give this man next to them His proper due. What could he possibly have lost by submitting, in those final moments of his life, to the Lordship of Jesus? By not submitting, he lost everything. To this day and forever, he has to be regretting his arrogant miscalculation.

Waiting until the last minute for anything is almost always risky. Many of us will never have the precarious luxury of a last-minute, life-saving opportunity like that afforded the two thieves at Calvary. Even if we did, chances are, we'd self-righteously blow that chance, too.

The most important decision you will ever make in your life is what to do with that extraordinary man who hanged on the middle cross. What a tragedy that some of us take the most critical decision of our lives so lightly or don't attend to it at all.

Being Deceived, the Worst Kind of Tragedy

If you ever have to do time in hell, that will be an eternity without parole. It is indescribably worse than if you simply died and that were the end of it. No one can pray you, buy you, bail you, or plea bargain you out of there. And if anyone has misled you into believing that you can secure your destiny in heaven by selecting from some convenient palatable menu of "higher powers," forget it.

That consoling bit of false information is one of the most malevolent acts of kindness anyone could ever offer you. If anyone offers you spirituality without walking you to Calvary and introducing you to Jesus, they've simply painted the road to hell in blurred, deceptive Technicolor.

There Is Only One Way

There are many "higher powers," but there is only one Jesus and only one way. There is also only one instruction manual: the Bible. Read it. If you don't read another book in your life, read that one. If you don't even finish reading the book you have in your hands right now, read that one. It contains the only available blueprint for putting true meaning into your life, taking the sting out of death, and obtaining a free full guarantee of an eternity in heaven. If you don't know where to start, let me suggest Acts 16:31 and Romans 10:9: "Believe on the Lord Jesus Christ, and thou shalt be saved, and thy house"; "That if thou shalt confess with thy mouth the Lord Jesus, and shalt believe in thine heart that God hath raised him from the dead, thou shalt be saved." There are other biblical references with similar simple instructions for being saved *from* hell and *for* heaven. But if you only follow the instructions in these two verses, you have already found the path to the cross. Go there, drop to your knees, and pray this little prayer that will change your life for all eternity:

> *Dear Jesus. I don't even know You, but I know You know me. I'm not sure I even love you, but I know you love me. I'm here at the cross, and I know that God sent You, His only Son, to die here so I, a sinner, can be saved. I accept Your gift, and I thank You from the*

bottom of my heart. On second thought, I do
love You. Amen.

Now, just as surely as if you had walked up to an airline ticket counter and walked away with a plane ticket in your hand, if you followed those instructions and prayed that prayer, you have your ticket to heaven. You have walked to the cross, and with a nail-pierced hand, Jesus has given you your ticket. It is really that simple.

The next logical question is, "Really now, how much is this ticket going to cost me?"

2

THE COST

For the wages of sin is death;
but the gift of God is eternal life
through Jesus Christ our Lord.

ROMANS 6:23

We are all issued a ticket to hell when we are born, simply by being a descendant of Adam. According to the *Liberty Bible Commentary*, "One act of disobedience to God [the eating of the forbidden apple in the Garden of Eden] was sufficient to allow sin to enter and permeate the entire realm of humanity." That inherited ticket to the valley of the damned will cost you everything, including your life, unless you surrender it at the cross. There, absolutely free, you can exchange it for a ticket to heaven. Two thousand years ago, Jesus shed His blood and gave His life on that cross to buy enough tickets for everyone who asks. It sounds too good to be true, too easy to be authentic. If it really is free there must be a hitch.

The Hitch

I finally did it. After living over half a normal lifetime and vowing I'd never do it, I finally took the computer plunge. I did a 180-degree conversion from no tech to so much tech I have no idea what to do with it all. I have no question that I made the right decision, but now I must decide how I want to manage all this potential. I can peck away at the computer keyboard and get this book written, taking advantage of only the most basic features available on this magnificent piece of equipment. Or I can set out to milk and master every minute detail, vastly improving the worth and quality of my decision. I've opted for the latter.

A similar choice is yours. The rest of this book

is about how to live after you've locked in your reservation for heaven. You can simply plop yourself down and bask in the comfort of knowing you're on the right road and leave it at that. Or you can devour the instruction manual, hang close to its author, polish your prayer life, and start growing up—spiritually. I hope you'll choose the latter.

Spiritual laziness has its risks. God has an infinite cache of armor and ammunition to help you win against Satan's fiery darts. But the battle is often fierce and unrelenting, and the battlefield is no place to begin donning your fatigues and loading your shells. We are instructed in Ephesians 6:11-17 to "Put on the whole armour of God. . ." which includes "having your loins girt about with truth," "having on the breastplate of righteousness," "your feet shod with the preparation of the gospel of peace," and "taking the shield of faith. . . the helmet of salvation, and the sword of the Spirit, which is the Word of God."

If, in addition to reading God's Word, the Bible, you choose to continue reading this book, I will make every effort to reward your time with some good sense, good humor, and even a little bit of good mischief. Life on the road to heaven is pretty exacting and sometimes painful, but it doesn't need to be dull. And if we don't have the pleasure of personally meeting here on earth, I hope I'll meet you in heaven.

3

PRECISION: AN ENDANGERED ART

*It is easier for a camel to go through
the eye of a needle, than for a rich man
to enter ino the kingdom of God.*

MATTHEW 19:24, MARK 10:25, LUKE 18:25

Several years ago, I was listening to the evening news when a rather obscure item was briefly and blandly reported by one of the major news services. It struck me as a very important bit of news, but I never heard it again, nor have I seen it in print. Even though I have been unable to retrieve the original item, let me give it to you exactly as I remember it. I think it is still an important bit of news.

On that date several years ago, the Soviet Union sent a satellite into space where it safely reached its first orbit. Once it had stabilized, the ground crew issued instructions to the on-board computer to proceed to its next assigned orbit. Instead, the satellite blew up!

When the instructions were later reviewed, they were found to be flawless—well, *almost* flawless. There was one minor error in them that would be comparable to the insertion of an apostrophe where it didn't belong. Some people might call that a petty blunder, but it was that "petty blunder" that instructed the onboard computer to self-destruct rather than change orbits. Whoever floated that apostrophe had much more than a blunder on his conscience; he had an attitude problem, a serious attitude problem. When precision is required, "close enough" will not do.

Admittedly, much of life does not hang precariously by the thread of an apostrophe. If one is making a sand castle on the beach, for instance, it isn't necessary to count every grain of sand or every droplet of water. Or if you're baking a cake, you don't need to measure a perfectly calibrated cup of flour to wind up with a perfectly delicious piece of cake. Or even if you're remodeling a house and you cut a board a few millimeters short, the likelihood of that being a carpentry catastrophe is negligible.

But if you're really serious about getting to heaven, there is only one way—the way of the cross—and one name, Jesus. Nothing and no one else will do, no matter how rich or pious or powerfully persuasive you may be. On either of these two points—the way and the name—there is no room for error, even one as small and seemingly inconsequential as an apostrophe.

Are Some Things Really Either Right or Wrong?

I once had a poster in my office showing a little boy with every button on his jacket lined up with the wrong buttonhole. The caption read, "If you don't get the first button right, none of the rest of them will match up." Now for most little boys I know, that's no big deal. In fact, if it weren't for mamas and grandmas, I suspect many little jackets would never quite get lined up properly. And the little boys inside would be in no way diminished or demeaned by it.

But try dialing a phone number with a single wrong digit, or opening a lock with one number missing from the combination, or playing a violin with one string slightly off key. To really capture the frustration of imprecision, try solving a long and complicated math problem with one plus sign transposed to a minus. Every step in the calculation can be otherwise correct, but the answer will be wrong. In many instances, if something isn't exactly right, it's entirely wrong. There are no acceptable gradations of "partly right" in between. Upholding that precise standard can be a rather unpopular thing to do.

When Only "Right" Will Do

One of the psychological tests I use includes a subtest involving visual symbols that represent words. The representative symbols are then used to "write" sentences that must be read much like a foreign language. While some of the symbols are easier to remember than others, one is particularly troublesome—the symbol for "little." For some reason, many children will repeat "little" properly while learning the symbol system, but then substitute the word "small" when reading the test sentence.

Well, "small" is wrong! The only correct translation of that symbol is "little." Now that may sound like the splitting of hairs, but splitting and measuring hairs is the very point of this subtest. It's a point not very graciously received especially by little minds which have already been etched and scarred by the "close enough" syndrome, and for whom "little" and "small" are "the same thing!" They just don't get the meaning of "precise."

When the situation dictates that there is only one right answer to a question, however, or one correct way to perform a task, you simply state it and stick to it. Getting into an argument, even a civil discussion about it, can be misleading and unfair. There is nothing to be gained and much to be lost by giving children, and adults for that matter, the illusion that facts are negotiable. Some things simply require precision.

Rules Are Made to Be Followed

Many years ago, I performed my own rite of passage into the world of nonnegotiable facts when I was a senior nursing student at a now defunct hospital school of nursing. I was working the day shift and was in charge of medications, a responsibility I discharged with impeccable accuracy. By the time I handed a patient his pills, there was never a question about the fact that this was the right patient, and these were the right pills. Strict rules governed the dispensing of medications, and I precisely followed every one of them—well, nearly every one.

The charge nurse who relieved me for the evening shift was an alumnus of this well-regarded school, and she had graduated with the coveted gold star for her outstanding performance as a nurse. She and I had developed a relationship of mutual trust and respect, especially in matters where "exactly right" was the only right as in the dispensing of medicines. Every day when I checked the work schedule, if she were the nurse relieving me at the end of the shift, I would have all the four o'clock medications set up for her and ready to be distributed to patients. I was honored to do it, and she appreciated the help; we both benefited from the arrangement.

Until one day. . .I was about to walk off duty when I was approached by my nursing instructor. She had just made a supervisory inspection of the medication room, and her demeanor was very. . .supervisory. I sensed this was not going to be a friendly chat. She wondered if I knew anything about the medications —all set up by somebody and ready to be administered to patients by somebody else.

Now let me explain something. There is a strict inflexible safety rule regarding the administration of medications. It is akin to the "Did-you-pack-your-own-bags?" rule now imposed on every airline passenger at every airport in the world. If you didn't pack your own bags, don't put them on the plane. They may contain a bomb. The medical version of that rule is, "Did you set up the medications yourself?" If you didn't, don't distribute them. They may contain an error. The little scheme I shared with the charge nurse was a serious violation of that safety rule.

My instructor was now approaching a sensitive nerve in me, the one touching my attitude. You see, I was a crackerjack student nurse, and I didn't *make* medication mistakes. I didn't need that rule. And the outstanding nurse coming on duty had earned the gold star and she didn't *permit* medication mistakes. She didn't need that rule either. We had an arrangement made in hospital heaven, and I, at least, was not ready to let some earthling sabotage it.

Well, that dear instructor of mine helped me get over my attitude really fast. I meekly slipped back into the medication room to execute a correction. One by one, I began pouring the pills back into their respective bottles.

The next thing I knew, there were two of us in the medication room. That was one more than I had counted on and one more than there was room for. I didn't even bother to look up because I recognized the supervisory demeanor, and I smelled the aroma of outrage. Both were stifling.

Unfortunately, another cardinal rule applies to the dispensing of medicines: You *never* return a pill or a liquid to the supply bottle for redispensing. If you do, the integrity of the medication in that supply bottle is compromised. This was an even more serious safety violation than the one I was trying to correct.

You can probably appreciate the fact that, by

now, I wasn't fully registering all the finer details of this nightmare. I simply had no way out of the mess I was in without making things messier, and I had already done enough of that. Now it was I who needed a dose of redemption.

Redemption always has its price. When someone transgresses, someone needs to pay. I will probably never fully know the cost of my redemption that day. Whatever it was, my supervisor paid it. I do know that it was one of the most humbling and defining experiences of my life and particularly of my nursing career. My respect for that exacting, yet compassionate instructor rose by many notches because of it. It was a lesson in precision I will never forget and have never had to repeat.

Let me return now to the title of this book, *Heaven*. If you research the word "heaven" on the Internet, you will find an odd potpourri of 187,841 matches ranging from serious to sacrilegious to downright bizarre. If you pursue long enough, you will find an occasional match that refers to a specific biblical reference, but that is rare. Most of the entries reflect a tangled conglomeration of bohemian theology, mantralike lyrics, sad suicidal pleas, heaven sightings, heaven jokes, heaven maps, and endless chatroom exchanges among sincere heaven enthusiasts.

As diverse and tasteless as many of these thousands of Internet entries are, they all have one common thread, either explicit or implied, that is fundamentally biblical, well, sort of biblical: heaven is the opposite of hell, and heaven, any heaven, is the better of the two.

While there may be some defensible logic in that, it completely misses the illogical, indefensible point that there is only one heaven, only one way, and only one reliable reference for getting the route straight. We've got God's word on it. When God says something, you don't defend it; you just believe it. If it's an instruction, you just do it. When it's a road map to heaven, you follow it precisely. And if you haven't learned to respect the importance of being precise, there is no way in the world to wind up in heaven. The truth is, the only other place to wind up is hell. There is truly no greater tragedy in all the world than winding up lost in hell—forever—hopelessly, abysmally, irreversibly forever.

Hell is what is in store for all of us if we do nothing. It is also what is in store for all of us if we do the right thing, even a whole lot of the right thing, if we have not first met Jesus at the cross and transferred off the road to hell and onto the highway to heaven.

We can diligently obey the law, give generously to help others, slow down the speed of life, stand alone against the world if necessary, burn a thousand candles, pray a zillion prayers, attend church regularly, love our neighbor, even read the entire Bible—but sadly, that will not get us to heaven. We must meet Jesus at the cross where the only acceptable posture is on our knees, where the only verdict is "pardoned," and the only cost is free.

If you are the kind of person who wants to write your own ticket, pay your own way, set your own rules, and even argue your own case, the very simplicity and lowliness of God's gift of salvation may put you off. Don't allow that to happen.

Heaven and hell are for real, and heaven truly is the opposite of hell. But not just any heaven will do. To paraphrase Shakespeare, hell by any other name, even some fabricated version of heaven, is still hell. There is nothing to gain—except perhaps some temporary and dubious pleasure—and everything to lose, by disparaging the sanctity of heaven and minimizing the horrors of hell. On the other hand, there is every-thing to gain and nothing to lose, except perhaps also some temporary and dubious pleasure, by following God's divine design for admission to heaven.

Heaven is one of the most popular subjects of the entire Bible. It is referred to 583 times in 51 of the 66 books in the King James Version. Many of these refer-ences simply include the word "heaven" and don't give a clue about how to get there. They are just reminders of the reality and importance of heaven and serve to keep the glorious hope of heaven eternally alive.

Some of the references, however, give very specific directions for getting there. These directions were not designed by a committee; they were not agreed upon in a high-level summit nor written in politically cor-rect terms, and they are subject neither to negotiation nor change. They must simply be followed. Heaven depends on it, and for anything less, there is hell to pay. There is no greater reward than heaven and no higher price tag than hell.

Failure to Do It Right Is Not Just a Private Affair

A couple of years ago, November of 1996 to be exact, I, along with two busloads of other Holy Land pilgrims, was chomping at the bit to cross the border from Israel into Jordan and prepare for the long and arduous hike into Petra. Petra is a two thousand-year-old impenetrable fortress in southern Jordan built during the time of Christ out of red sandstone. It is referred to as the "Rose-Red City" because of the deep color of the rock. There is only one entrance to Petra, and the path leading to it is a kilometer-long, narrow gorge with majestic rock formations rising two hundred meters in spots. Many of us on the tour had waited a lifetime to visit this awesome place, and the wait at the border was beginning to feel ominous.

Our tour leader finally entered the bus to announce that one of our group had left his passport at the hotel in Tiberias, where we all had checked out a few hours earlier. That passport was the ticket to Jordan and thus to Petra. That gentleman was a bona fide member of our group, and he knew the rules for entering Jordan. Like all the rest of us, he had the instruction manual long in advance of this trip to prevent

just such an incident as this. There were many pass-
ports on those two buses at that moment, but not one
of them would do for him; he needed his own.

By the time we learned of the dilemma, the hotel
in Tiberias had already been contacted, the missing
passport had been located, and a courier was speeding along the route we had just traveled to deliver the
document. Several hours and a generous dose of
benevolence later, the passport was again in the
hands of its owner. Now, with all of us duly creden-
tialed, the gates to Jordan were finally opened, and
we crossed over together.

I was reminded of a story in Matthew 25 in
which Jesus told His disciples about ten virgins, five
of whom also failed to follow the rules. I was struck
by some of the parallels and some of the critical dif-
ferences between that parable and the experience we
had just had at the Jordanian border. The virgins in
Matthew were all going to the same place, a wedding,
to meet the bridegroom; they were the bridegroom's
attendants. Five of them wisely took not only their
lamps but oil enough to keep them burning. The
other five were foolish and took only their lamps but
no extra oil. When the bridegroom arrived, and it

was time to go in to the wedding, the five wise virgins entered with their lamps burning brightly. The five foolish ones had run out of oil and had to go shopping to get some more. They didn't make it back in time to enter the festivities before the doors were shut—forever. There was no second chance, no waiver of the entry requirements, no courier to bail them out and bring more oil and no waiting for them by those who had prepared properly. Late was late, whether it was thirty seconds, thirty minutes, or thirty hours late. Once the bridegroom arrived, all options were gone. If you weren't ready, you didn't get in. It was that simple.

The "foolish virgin" in our group was dealt a more compassionate hand. His "lamp oil" was delivered, the gates to Jordan were held open until his documents were in place, and the group he was with—two busloads of us—waited until he readied himself so we could all enter Jordan together. When someone transgresses, someone needs to pay, and we all paid a price that day for this man's imprecision. Had justice been served, he would have been left behind.

When it comes to heaven, unfortunately many *will* be left behind. (See Matthew 7:14.) We all have only one lifetime within which to get it right—exactly right. When we come to the end of that lifetime, we will enter eternity, either an eternity in heaven or an eternity in hell. There are no reruns.

There is also precious little time. If you are a Christian, your eyes should be looking up, and your ears should be listening for the sound of trumpets getting in tune. When God Almighty finally lifts His baton, the musicians of heaven will perform His majestic score and "in the twinkling of an eye," Christians will be gone—to heaven—forever.

If you are not a Christian, you lose nothing by checking out the cross and comparing the costs. The road to hell may make you feel like a millionaire, but it will ultimately bankrupt you forever. The road to heaven, on the other hand, has no admission fee, and the prize at the end has no equal. As Oswald Chambers points out, the reason it is so easy to obtain salvation is that it cost God so much. He gave His only Son for it. The reason it is so hard to accept salvation is because it *is* so easy.

For this one time in your life, if it sounds too good to be true—believe it!

The Assignment

1. Find and follow the directions for the trip to
   heaven. Here's a start:
   John 3:16, 36
   John 5:24
   John 6:47
   Acts 4:12
   Acts 16:31
   Romans 10:9, 13

2. Get a little taste of heaven from the architect:
   Read Revelation 21 for a description.
   Read John 14:1–3 for Jesus' promise that He'll
   be back to escort those who have followed
   the directions to the place He has been
   preparing for over two thousand years.
   What a mansion that must be!

4

STAND FIRM—
BUT CHECK THE TURF FIRST

Wherefore take unto you the whole armour of God,
that ye may be able to withstand in the evil day,
and having done all, to stand.

EPHESIANS 6:13

For years I had a poster in my office showing a vast lifeless desert with a single flower growing out of the sand. The caption read, "Never be afraid to stand alone." That poster served as a daily reminder to me and a frequent encouragement to many people I counseled that standing alone may be lonely, but standing in the middle of a misguided crowd, or holding to a popular but ill-advised point of view, is of little comfort either. There is also no heroism in standing for or against something, only to cut loose from it under pressure.

When you place your footing in the Bible, you are standing firmly on God's Word, and you never need to be afraid to stand alone.

Standing Lonely

Years before I put that poster on the wall, I attended a concert with my father, during which the "Hallelujah Chorus" was sung. For some strange reason the conductor announced to the audience that we could stand up or not while it was played. As you probably know, tradition requires the audience to stand during the presentation of the Hallelujah Chorus because Handel wrote this part of *The Messiah* expressly to honor the King of Kings and Lord of lords! Even King George, at the London premiere of *The Messiah,* spontaneously stood when the "Hallelujah Chorus" was performed, he was so moved by it.

No one stood. Then I saw my Dad rise boldly to his feet, all alone. I remember thinking to myself, *Oh, Daddy, please don't do this!* But then I rose to stand with him. Another friend was sitting behind us. He also rose. In that crowd of well over a thousand people, we three stood alone to honor our king.

We had not stood thoughtlessly or apologetically, and certainly we were not on our feet to impress this intimidating crowd. We stood reverently and in worship, and a whirlwind of boos could not have brought us down. In those holy moments, as we listened to the heavenly hallelujah strains, we were aware of only the king. We were paying homage to Him.

Now mind you, there is no particular virtue in standing firmly and boldly out of sheer stubbornness. In fact, being around people who've never learned this can be quite unpleasant. They're the ones who twist every conversation into a debate and vehemently defend viewpoints they don't even believe in. Or they may be simply rugged individualists who haven't yet learned that compromise is sometimes nobler than confrontation.

His Word Never Changes

Return for a moment to chapter 2 and the specific armor God provides for helping us hold our ground on issues of eternal importance. The last item in that inventory is the Sword of the Spirit, or the Bible. If you're going to stake your reputation on a position, especially if you must defend that position all by yourself, make sure you have first defined your position according to the unchanging Word of God.

Many Words Do Change

There *is* virtue in standing firm in your convictions regarding right versus wrong and good versus bad. We are living at a time when some people seem to have an aversion to these moral and ethical distinctions. Many refuse to use such antithetical terms at all, simply accepting the notion that what qualified as wrong yesterday may become strangely right today, and what was genius yesterday may be politically incorrect today. Sometimes you want to cry out, "Would someone please stop messing with my words?"

Words, you see, are critical. When language becomes adulterated, a black and white issue can suddenly turn gray, simply by using different words to describe it. I might be vehemently opposed to an idea or a behavior today, only to find that tomorrow's description of it sounds quite acceptable. On the contrary, I might sanction a behavior today and find myself on the other side of it tomorrow.

Take cheating, for example. Cheating was once considered an academic disgrace. In some public school systems across America, it now comes under the benevolent umbrella of "cooperative learning." Laziness and irresponsibility, which used to spawn parental reproach, sometimes now garner services for the handicapped, depriving the certifiably handicapped of needed services. Abortion, once synonymous with murder, is now more acceptable than disturbing a bird's nest. Homosexuality, which not too many years ago was a treatable, psychiatric disorder, is now a politically powerful alternative lifestyle.

Praying and reading from the Bible in a public school used to be part of the normal school day's activities. Now it has been transformed into a constitutional sin. For generations, displaying the Nativity scene and singing Christmas carols on public property at Christmastime was as natural as breathing. Now even breathing the word "Christ" in relation to *Christ*mas has become an anathema in many previously amiable circles. Along similar lines, common courtesies on the highway, such as letting a waiting vehicle into a tight line of traffic, which were once applauded, now often engender "road rage" in the already inconvenienced and impatient.

The point is, if cheating, for example, is inherently wrong, then it continues to be wrong even after it sounds right. Conversely, if prayer and Bible reading in public schools was constitutionally sound in the past, then the wise thing to do would be to reread the Constitution rather than stop reading the Bible.

Many issues in life are simply matters of taste or cultural preference or even convenience. Standing alone against a saber-rattling world on those issues can be a rather dubious expenditure of time and energy. Other matters, however, are clearly defined in God's word and anything other than support of those biblically defined principles would be a serious ethical compromise. Before stepping out alone for or against something, spend time in God's Word. Take up the Sword of the Spirit.

One Woman's Quest for Terra Firma

You may never have heard of her, but her name is Bilquis Sheikh, and her life is now in jeopardy because of her discovery that the Bible is God's only Word and the God of the Bible is the only true God.

One day many years ago, Madame Sheikh reached for the two books she kept on her bedside table, the Bible and the Koran. She held one in each hand and asked God a question.

"Which, Father, which one is Your book?"

Then, as surely as if He were answering her audibly, He asked her a question.

"In which book do you meet Me as your Father?"

She answered, "In the Bible."

From that moment, she knew she had finally found the one true God. You see, her Muslim god, Allah, does not enjoy that unique distinction of being "Father." Nor does any other god of any other religion have that distinction. It is no linguistic coincidence that the Lord's Prayer begins with, "Our Father, Who art in heaven. . . ." God's Son, Jesus, taught us to pray this way.

When you have that life-changing encounter with Jesus at the cross, you meet God as Father. Then you also know you can stake your life, if necessary, on everything He has to say in His Word, the Holy Bible.

There is much more to Bilquis Sheikh's story about her subsequent donning of God's armor and her firm stand on the unshakeable ground established in His Word. She has written this story in a book entitled, *I Dared to Call Him Father*. Madame Sheikh risked her life in defense of the One who gave His own life so we can all "dare to call Him Father."

When "Terra" Is Not "Firma"

On a recent tour of the Louisiana bayous, I observed a vast, lush swamp that, on the surface, gave no hint of what was beneath it. Our guide cautioned that one step out of the boat onto the inviting turf was not recommended. Over the years, the ground underneath this floating trap had gradually washed away and even a sincere, seasoned wilderness-survivor would quickly sink.

The convictions of many are the same way. Actually, the word "conviction" is much too respectable a term to describe what is trumpeted today and relinquished tomorrow, or what you swear by today and toss out tomorrow. That is more accurately a "whim," and whims are very easy to come by. It is much more difficult to find someone—or be someone—who believes in something today, which they believed in yesterday and may even need to die for tomorrow.

I am often inspired by an unusual prerequisite for singing with the original Robert Shaw Chorale: Every singer had to be a soloist. A group composed of soloists, whether in music or in discourse, is one strong collective voice. At any moment, any individual might be called upon to sing alone or stand alone and only a "soloist" is up to the challenge. There is nothing wrong with savoring the support of colleagues in the musical rendition of *The Messiah* or in the courtroom defense of your convictions. But those supports are sometimes not there, and whether or not you independently step forward and sing your solo or defend your beliefs will be largely determined by how well you have done your homework.

The Assignment

The Word of God, the Bible, is absolutely reliable. It is just as reliable today as it was yesterday and will be tomorrow. Read it. Memorize it. Believe it. Stand firmly on the immutable principles in it. Start living them until they become as automatic and habitual as breathing.

Brace yourself for those times when you may need to stand alone against your whole world, in support of those principles. To survive as a soloist, you must work on this assignment for the rest of your life. But remember, not one part of this assignment will qualify you for heaven unless you have first met Jesus at Calvary and accepted His free unlimited offer to be your Savior.

5

PRAY. . . . A TALL ORDER

Pray one for another.
JAMES 5:16

Pray without ceasing.
I THESSALONIANS 5:17

Prayer is one of the most universally popular activities, and that fact should be one to celebrate. It is the topic of more discussion groups, the subject of more books, the title of more courses of study, and occupies more of people's time than almost any other single issue. Simply defined, it is a conversation with Jesus. But that is where the problem often lies and the celebration often stops. So many people pray without being in any way connected to Jesus.

The Connection

One day I was standing near some pay phones in a department store when a young man stepped up to one of them, grabbed the receiver, and started talking animatedly into the mouthpiece. Soon he was augmenting this conversation with hand gestures, facial expressions, and body language befitting a seasoned actor. It suddenly occurred to me that he had put no money into the phone, and obviously he had no live communication line to anyone. I wondered to myself, "Does he really think someone is listening to him at the other end of that line? And is he going to hang up the receiver expecting something dramatic to happen as a result of this conversation?"

While everything he said may have made perfect sense, his requests may have been legitimate, he may have been convinced someone out there was listening and would respond, still he had done nothing to establish a connection. Without a connection, he was simply talking to himself. The sad thing about prayer is that so many people are just talking to themselves. They have never connected with Jesus, and Jesus is the communication line to God. There is no other way to connect to God.

One can talk forever to some generic god, hug trees, touch rocks, assume pious positions, chant mantras, spin wheels, all to no avail. If we have not made that life-changing journey to the cross, our prayers are as empty and meaningless as that poor fellow's phone conversation.

Nudged to Pray

It was the middle of the night, and I was the charge nurse on the medical floor of a hospital in my hometown, a town where everybody knows everybody. On this particular night, a lady I knew lay dying, and I did not want to see her or deal with her death. In fact, she was a lady of some prominence and prestige, and I was intimidated by even her slumbering presence.

As I made my rounds with my flashlight, I was ever so careful not to awaken her, even as I dutifully made sure she was breathing and was showing no signs of imminent demise. All night long, I felt this nudge that I should go in there and talk with her, pray with her, hold her hand, talk with her about Jesus; instead I tiptoed in and out without even touching her bed, lest even a slight vibration disturb her sleep.

In the morning, I gave my report to the day staff, left for home, and tried to forget, or worse yet, rationalize what I had done. I so vividly remember reminding God that He had put this lady in the company of saints for years, and surely they must have done their saintly duty. And if they hadn't, it wasn't my job to do it for them. And even if it were, He hadn't equipped me with the stature to reach such a celebrated, prominent, even pompous socialite as this. I thought of everything I could muster to quell the guilt that disturbed my sleep that day, but nothing worked very well.

The next day I read in the paper that she had died. Then—I nearly died. I had done a lot of praying the night before, mostly asking God to let me off the hook on this one. Now I remembered that I had forgotten to pray for *her*. That was many years ago, and she has been on my conscience ever since. I hope someone else in her life was more faithful than I, and I trust I will see her in heaven someday. I owe her an apology.

There Is Redemption

Several years later, I had another friend. This one was also prominent; in fact, he was a giant of a man in his profession. I had long since gotten over being intimidated by anyone God placed in my path, and this man and I had an easy, honest, heart-warming relationship.

The best part of that relationship was our conversations. Sometimes they were also the worst part. Almost every one, sooner or later, gravitated toward discussions about God, and then, if I felt really brave, I would bring up the subject of Jesus.

My friend felt pretty good about God. He had this notion that he and God were colleagues of sorts. But Jesus? He was another matter. Jesus was a man, not even a very desirable man at that, in my friend's opinion. In fact, the name of Jesus took a real beating in some of our conversations. Sometimes I wondered if my friend was trying to crucify Him all over again.

For this man, I did remember to pray. . .and pray and pray and pray. Without ceasing, I prayed.

One Sunday when our pastor at church asked us to bow our heads and pray for one specific person, this man was the one I prayed for. As I entered my house after church that day, the phone was ringing. It was my friend, and I informed him I had just come from church. He immediately asked, "Did you pray for me?" For the first time ever, I heard sincerity rather than sarcasm in his voice as he asked that question. So I told him the whole story of the pastor's request, my prayer, and my hope that he had listened to whatever God was trying to tell him.

That was the last serious conversation he and I ever had. Shortly thereafter, he went into a cardiac crisis, had emergency surgery, and died several days later. Somewhere between our conversation and his death, I feel certain he made that decisive trek to the cross, not because of me, but because God answers prayer. And I really believe that if God nudges you to pray for someone's salvation, He intends to somehow nudge that person all the way to the cross.

Prayer Doesn't Change "Things"

Oswald Chambers once wrote, "It is not so true that 'prayer changes things' as that prayer changes *me* and I change things." I was blessed to be born to praying parents, and their prayers, along with those of many others, have changed me. I regret that I cannot rewrite the story about my patient whom I let down. But partly because of that story, I could write this second one. I have learned that when God prompts me to pray for someone or about something, I'd better pray. If I don't, He'll find someone else who will. But then, He just has to keep working on me until I finally learn to pray. I cannot walk with Jesus and not pray.

Dr. Wim Malgo, in his excellent book *Called to Pray*, says, "If God has told us that we should pray, three things are necessary for us: first, prayer; second, prayer; and third, prayer!" It is so tempting to approach prayer as a topic for group discussion, an exercise in meditation, a theme for a computer search, or a college course we feel duty-bound to take. While prayer may be all of these, our activities are of no worth whatsoever if we do not stop talking about prayer and start praying. We may be tempted to pray as though we were reading a book: pray, close the cover, and be done with it. But that misses the whole point of praying:

Answers!

Charles Spurgeon once wrote, "We should expect answers to prayer and should not be easy without them any more than we should be if we had written a letter to a friend about important business and had received no reply." God does answer prayer. Sometimes those answers are so dramatic we want to shout them from the rooftops, like when someone prays for healing and they become well. Many answers are more subdued, like when we pray for a safe trip and then arrive at our destination without incident. Even more obscure are those answers we never see or hear. And the most difficult answers of all are those that don't come even close to what we prayed for but are God's answers nonetheless.

Air in a Prayer

One night a number of years ago while I was in Pakistan, a friend and I decided to dine on Chinese fare rather than the usual Pakistani cuisine served in the campus dining room. We signed out the college car, made a reservation, and off we went to a suburb of Lahore called Gulberg. And Chinese fare deluxe we had!

While our trip to the restaurant was in daylight, our trip home began in the dark. No problem. With our stomachs full and our trusty car waiting, we got in and started back to Kinnaird Campus. About a mile into the trip, however, we both began to hear and feel the sound of trouble—a tire going flat.

Now that may not be a big deal in some parts of the world, but let me paint you our scene: Two women alone in a Muslim country without a chaperone, miles away from anybody or any abode, pitch dark and no flashlight, and the discovery, upon a fleeting, fearful inspection, that one tire had lost most of its air. It wasn't a pretty scene.

We quickly got back into the car, locked the doors, and prayed. Man, did we pray! Then, with faith the size of a molecule inside a mustard seed, we took off. Neither of us said a word. There were no words for these moments, just an anxious silence. Before we had time to fully comprehend our predicament, we had reached the locked gates of our campus.

At that instant, we both felt it: The tire flattened! We sat there in disbelief. We also sat in awe of the miracle we had just lived through. Later we discovered a large puncture wound in the tire; only a farfetched logic could possibly explain how it held just enough air that night just long enough for us to return safely to our campus.

Maybe prayer does change things. As we got out of the car, we saw the guard waiting to admit us. Whether prayer changes things or changes us suddenly became a moot point.

Pray Without Ceasing

We are required to do few things in life literally without stopping; breathing is one of them. If we stop breathing, we die. There are very few things in the Christian life we are required to do without stopping either; I think there is only one: praying. If we stop praying, our Christian life loses its vitality and it, too, dies.

The apostle Paul reminds us in 1 Thessalonians 5:17 that we are to "pray without ceasing." This is the very same Paul who, not long before he said that, was himself persecuting people who prayed. Not until God blinded and decked him on the road to Damascus did he finally decide to visit Calvary. This time he voluntarily fell flat on his face before the very man he had been persecuting. Somebody, somewhere, must have been praying for Paul, and God was answering. Strange and remarkable things happen to people who are being prayed for, and it isn't always cozy and comforting.

Unexpected Answers

Sometimes you may pray about something or someone and then stand back aghast as you watch the situation worsen or the person you prayed for fall apart. You may even wonder, as your own life begins to go into a tailspin, if you are being punished for praying.

That is one of the problems with praying: Sometimes God's answers don't seem to fit our prayers. At least they are sometimes not what we expected or wanted or even what we thought we were praying for.

Sixteen years ago my brother-in-law, an exceptionally cautious driver, was hit by a teenager driving to a local community college on very slippery roads. It was winter, and the young lady who hit him lost control of her car and slammed into him on the driver's side of his car. He received a severe head injury, and from that day he began a gradual process of neurological and motor decline. As a result of that injury, he had to retire early from a successful teaching career. He can no longer do simple routines like writing checks to pay bills or cutting the meat on his plate at mealtime or shaving without help. Also as a result of that injury, my sister has to continue to do all the work she did before his accident, in addition to all the work my brother-in-law used to do but no longer can.

To further complicate the situation, the young lady had barely minimum insurance on her car through a company that, in this case, was less than helpful. A lawsuit was eventually required to collect even enough money to cover his trips to and from the doctor. The situation was a disaster straight from hell—at least for sixteen years I had behaved as if it were.

I hardly knew the young lady who hit my brother-in-law, but I not only knew her parents, I drove past their house almost every day, saw them often on the street, watched them enjoy their grandchildren, and seethed inside every time our paths paralleled. I tried to make sure they never crossed.

This spring, a local group of senior citizens arranged a bus tour to Lancaster, Pennsylvania, to see the widely acclaimed production of *Noah*. When not enough people from Brookside Retirement Community signed up for the tour, it was opened to the public, and I made a reservation.

A couple weeks before departure time, we were all sent a list of people who would be going on the tour. When I received mine, I thought I would. . .get seasick! There on the list was this couple. I probably don't have to tell you that my mind went into spin mode, and I knew something would have to give. I was *not* (now God, you listen to me, I mean *not!*) going to sit on that bus, try to enjoy an otherwise spectacular show, and share umpteen meals in the company of those two people.

Well, that was all God needed to begin a major overhaul on me. Actually He had started the process some time before because I had already learned that, when faced with people you can't stand, don't like, don't even want to learn to like, you pray for them. And that is what I had done.

But before I went very far down that "kicking and screaming" road, I knew the real culprit here was me. Reluctantly, I started praying that God would either count me out of this trip or do something to my attitude. I just kept praying that prayer and figured God had enough time to perform some miracle before the trip, but I really did not expect one. I was not even sure I wanted one.

The day came for us to leave, and we were all invited to meet at 5:30 A.M. for coffee and donuts at the retirement community before starting out. I arrived early. So did that couple. The moment they entered, I knew something very special had happened. After sixteen years of strain and estrangement, it was as if we were meeting again for the first time. The brick wall of anger and bitterness and resentment had quietly crumbled during those two weeks I had prayed. I have no idea whether any change took place in them, or even if there needed to be one, but unknown to me, God had performed a miracle on my attitude.

We enjoyed our coffee and donuts together, and then everyone started boarding the bus. My roommate for this trip got on first and reserved our seat. When I got on a few minutes later, I could not believe my eyes. Sitting behind us was this couple. I knew then the battle was over, and the victory was won!

That battle will never need to be refought. Through it I learned that if you don't want something, don't pray for it. And if you do pray for it, expect it! I also learned that it is impossible to walk with Jesus and not pray. It is equally impossible to pray, I mean *really* pray, without walking with Jesus.

The Assignment

If you have not yet met Jesus at the cross, drop everything and go there. Then pray and pray and pray. If you *have* met Jesus at the cross, especially pray and pray and pray. Pray without ceasing.

6

SHHH. . .

Be still, and know that I am God.
PSALM 46:10

The story is told of a bishop and his friends who visited the home of a wealthy landowner in Illinois. After an elaborate and extravagant meal, the proud landowner took his guests to the roof balcony. There he pointed out to them that as far as they could see in every direction, he owned the land.

"There is one direction in which you haven't pointed," one of the guests noted.

"Which is that?" asked the host.

His guest pointed upward and asked, "How

much have you up there?"

The landowner soberly admitted, "I've been so busy I haven't had time to think about that."

It is no easy task to follow the instruction in Psalm 46:10 to "be still, and know that I am God." While some may argue the point, we really cannot know God in a life of constant busyness and relentless motion. Where there is motion, there is usually also noise. To really know God, we must be still. And to be still, we must slow the motion and quiet the noise.

I am under no illusions; I know this assignment is impossible for many people. They have families to care for, mouths to feed, bills to pay, schedules to keep, employers to satisfy, employees to nurture, mistakes to correct, and on and on and on. Everyone's list is different in content and length, but no one has a blank list. While one may prioritize the list, every task on it must sooner or later be done. Or at least the cost of leaving it undone is often too high even to consider.

The High Cost of Busy

Let me tell you something about the high cost of

busyness. My mother, who went to be with her Lord in 1992, spent the last several years of her life increasingly confined to a favorite chair, near a favorite window, savoring her favorite view, that of my dad returning home. He could have been returning from anywhere. It didn't matter as long as he was coming home.

My dad was a minister, and he was particularly sensitive and soothing among the sick. He made hospital visits within a radius of one hundred miles, day after day, week after week, and year after year. He was literally a phone call and a heartbeat away from anyone who needed pastoral comforting, day or night. Many decades before, my mom had put him out on loan to the Lord, never counting any personal cost.

My mother, on the other hand, was a voracious reader and had read the Bible, from Genesis to Revelation, over thirty times. She knew more about biblical Israel and the Jews than many Bible scholars do. She was also an encyclopedia of information about everything from history to geography to family genealogies. From cooking to canning to proper housekeeping. I think she knew all of Emily Post by heart and much more. When, in response to my frequent questions, she denied being lonely, she was probably being honest, although I often wondered if she were just trying to protect me from a painful truth.

The fact is, my mom had every reason to be lonely and often asked me to sit down and talk with her or come for a meal or review points in a book she was reading or play Scrabble or share some other activity with her, for which I was usually too busy. I have learned that the cost of "too busy" is very high, and I will be in debt for that cost for the rest of my life. I missed out on so much of my mother's wisdom and cooking and humor and love, for which there is no earthly substitute. Only the grace of God can lift the guilt that busyness has left in the pit of my stomach and replace the loss it has left in the center of my life.

Busyness has a way of creeping up on you, slowly, insidiously, often without fanfare and usually with your enthusiastic consent. By the time you are aware of the wildly accelerating tempo of your life, you are irrevocably committed.

One thing is certain; we are not born busy. That is something we learn. Anything learned has some-where, somehow been taught. And while anything learned can be unlearned, it is far better and easier to teach a loftier lifestyle to begin with. But if you find yourself already hopelessly committed and overbusy, you may be surprised if someday God steps in and slows down your free fall with a parachute.

Parachutes

A number of years ago I arrived at Kathmandu airport to visit friends. Unknown to me, as our plane landed, my friends took a picture. It wasn't until I looked at that photo that I realized a parachute had been deployed at the rear of our plane upon landing, to slow us down. I then learned that all large planes landing in Kathmandu are required to do the same thing. The planes' speed is so fast that without this extra help in slowing down, they would overshoot the runway and crash into the Himalayas that encircle the airport.

Many years ago God mercifully pulled the ripcord on *my* parachute and shifted one of the reckless areas of my life into slow gear. In a matter of just a few weeks I was issued so many speeding tickets I was destined to be denied the privilege of driving. I justified my driving speed with the argument that I was a nurse, often on call for emergency duty in the operating room, sometimes having to cover many miles to help save a life, and on and on. It didn't take long for a judge, who valued the sanctity of life, to remind me that I could easily end up taking someone else's life.

Chagrined and penitent, I made a solemn commitment to slow down in exchange for keeping my driver's license. I wish I could tell you I have never broken that commitment, but I cannot. I *can* tell you, however, that the speed of my whole life changed after that; I gained a new respect for the value of slowing down.

When Busy Becomes Too Busy

One of the most effective deterrents to spiritual health and growing in "the nurture and admonition of the Lord" (Ephesians 6:4) is busyness. Have you ever tried talking with someone whose attention you simply didn't have and whose mind was preoccupied? Or tried nabbing a few precious moments from someone who had none to spare? Or reached out to touch someone and their "line" was always busy?

I am not describing the exception, as lamentable as that would be. Unfortunately, more people are trapped in this hopeless, frenzied cycle of never ending things to do, than are not. That might be considered relatively inconsequential except for those eight compelling little words in Psalm 46:10: "Be still, and know that I am God. . . ." There is simply no way to spend time with Jesus and pay homage to Almighty God in a day where all the time slots are otherwise filled, and all the sensory modalities are overloaded and red hot. Don't expect to find God in that abysmal mess—not because He isn't there (He's everywhere), but because you'll be too busy and too distracted to notice. You have to be still to notice.

John Wesley White once described God as "a perfect gentleman." God never storms His way into your life without your permission. However, His Son, Jesus, stands ready at any moment to enter the opened door of every welcoming heart, from the most wholesome to the most depraved. He is on the outside of both hearts unless specifically invited in, and both are equally in need of God's gift of salvation. Entering eternity, having missed this guest's presence, is the greatest tragedy imaginable. If you've never slowed down long enough for God to get your attention—I mean *really* get it—it's time to start applying the brakes.

Someone once said, "To obtain maximum attention, it's hard to beat a good, big mistake." God never makes mistakes, but sometimes He permits unpleasant and tragic events to enter our lives to get our attention. These are often perceived as mistakes, and God is blamed for them. But if you haven't given Him your attention and slowed down otherwise, don't be surprised if you find yourself needing to turn to Him because "it hurts too much to cry," and because your tunnel has neither a light nor an end. Let me give you a piece of experienced advice: Don't wait for that!

Are You Dying to Live?

One day at work several years ago, someone placed a magazine clipping in my mailbox with the following anonymous somber reflection:

> First I was dying to finish high school
>   and start college.
> And then I was dying to finish college

and start working.
And then I was dying to marry
and have children.
And then I was dying for my children to
grow old enough so I could return
to work.
And then I was dying to retire.
And now, I am dying. . .
And suddenly I realize I forgot to live.

Listen up! Don't wait for death to get your attention!

When It's Too Hot to Move

In the late '60s, I spent a year in Pakistan where every day during the summer months life stops around 1:00 P.M. I mean it really stops, for about three hours. It is just too hot to move, much less work.

One day, I had gone into town and had not yet comprehended the full impact of the midday heat. I leisurely walked through my list of things I'd come to town to do and then leisurely searched for a tonga to get me home. A tonga, by the way, is a two-wheeled cart with a driver and a horse.

Well, there were plenty of tongas, and as I saw them lined up along the curb, I thought to myself, *Wow! I'm in luck!*

Wrong! I soon found out that my need to get home was no match for any of those drivers' need for sleep. I managed to awaken one of them—but then I wished I hadn't.

I am still wondering if anything, any earthshaking thing, could interrupt their quiet time. Probably not.

But I had learned an invaluable lesson about quiet time from those tonga drivers. There is something almost sacred about it, even when it has no spiritual or particularly religious significance. To be honest, I am not nearly so strict in guarding my "alone-with-God" time as those men were in protecting their need to nap. I am still working on improving my quiet God-time.

A Caveat

I never discuss a few subjects without a caveat; "slowing down" is one of them. Although we're living in an age of unprecedented speed complicated by confusion and chaos, there are still some people whose only gear in life is "park." They park in front of the TV, mesmerized by soaps and frenzied by sports; they park in the church pew trying to absorb enough "religion" to float them through another week; they park in the classroom and do just enough homework to receive a complimentary "pass." When called upon to shift gears, they merely find another parking spot. To those people I offer this caution: If what you have just read is in any way misconstrued as an affirmation of that barren lifestyle, I have been misread.

Too Fast: A Common Malady

Unless you have been granted some providential immunity, your name is likely on the roster of those driving through life too fast. And unless you have some sense that slowing down your life right now is preferable to speeding up, you will probably not want to tackle this assignment. But here it is!

The Assignment

Starting with Psalm 46:10, "Be still, and know that I am God. . . ," find as many references as you can which in any way relate to the need to slow down. Here's a start: 2 Timothy 2:15, "Study to show thyself approved unto God . . ."; 1 Thessalonians 5:17, "Pray without ceasing"; Proverbs 15:16, "Better is little with the fear of the LORD than great treasure and trouble therewith." There are many more, and some may speak to *your* need to slow down but not necessarily to someone else's. Remember, this is *your* assignment.

Guard this study time with the conviction of those tonga drivers. Should someone or something interrupt, only you can decide if the interrupting need exceeds your need to be uncompromisingly alone with God.

Now, begin a little at a time, to reduce your load— of work, worry, wasted time, crammed calendars, ruthless competition, and the relentless accumulation of *things*, many of which you probably neither need nor can afford. Start giving some of your quiet attention to God before He must activate the STOP button on your personal stopwatch in order to get it.

7

MAY I SERVE YOU?

Serve the LORD with gladness.
PSALM 100:2

You're probably thinking, *Aha, I knew there had to be a catch. No one gives away something without expecting something in return.* Well, that is almost true except for one thing: God is not just anyone. When He gave His only Son in atonement for our sins, He provided that gift absolutely free, with no strings attached, no debt to pay, no small print in which to hide a surprise price. The only thing we must do is willingly and deliberately accept His gift.

But when someone offers us a gift, and we accept

the offer and take the gift, it is common courtesy to show our gratitude in some way. The assurance of salvation and the promise of heaven is no ordinary gift, and it deserves some extraordinary expression of gratitude. Serving the Lord who gave the gift *is* that gratitude.

The idea of serving—serving God and serving others—is not a particularly popular twenty-first-century idea. But surely, if someone was willing to give His life for you and me, being able to serve Him in return should be an honor.

The "Master" Servant

Who would ever think that the all-powerful master whom we have the honor of serving would Himself become the model for servanthood? The apostle John, in John 13, tells about Jesus' last supper with His disciples before He was betrayed and crucified, at which He performed the most humble act imaginable. He took a towel, poured water into a basin, washed His disciples' feet, and wiped them dry.

Most people in Jesus' day wore sandals, and the

major mode of transportation was walking. Roads were unpaved and dusty, and according to custom, a family servant washed the tired, dust-covered feet of guests. So this ritual was not uncommon. The fact that Jesus Himself performed it is what made it so unusual. But no servants were at this private supper, only Jesus and His disciples. That was no oversight. Our Lord clearly intended to use this private occasion to make a public declaration about the importance of serving. After He washed the last disciple's feet, He said, "If I then, your Lord and Master, have washed your feet; ye also ought to wash one another's feet" (John 13:14).

Now I know that directive may sound a little too humbling for our twenty-first-century narcissistic mindset. But something wonderful happens on the way from simply eating the bread and drinking the wine at the Holy Communion table, to stooping and washing someone's feet.

I grew up in the Mennonite Church where footwashing was a part of every Communion service. Many of the young footwashers, like myself, chafed at this humbling ritual. We did it anyway and for many of us, the more we obediently performed the task, the more meaningful it became.

Whether one takes the matter of washing someone's feet literally or metaphorically, it takes on its real meaning in everyday acts of service to others. Sometimes those acts are brief, bland, even anonymous. Often no one even seems to notice. At other times they may be quite dramatic and long term. Either way, we are modeling Jesus' example. In the process of learning to appreciate the importance of that, I . . .

Almost Blew It!

While living and working in Rockland County, New York, in the mid-'60s, I spent a great deal of time at the Missionary Orientation Center in Stony Point, New York. One day during one of my visits there, I was approached about the need for a teacher of psychology at Kinnaird College for Women in Lahore, Pakistan, and was asked if I would be interested.

Immediately, I sensed that God was in this picture and that the position at Kinnaird College was more than just a job offer. I had been praying for an overseas position in psychology for months and knew the opportunities in that field with any church mission board would be limited. This was an answer to those prayers as surely as if it had been mailed to me in an envelope.

I knew almost nothing about Pakistan, nor was I a member of the denomination seeking to fill the post. Besides, I had a contract to honor with the North Rockland Public School System, and I had no reason to want to break it.

But I applied. I was accepted, and I corresponded with the principal of Kinnaird College and the psychology professor I would be replacing. I received photos of the beautiful Kinnaird Campus and read everything I could get my hands on about the country and the college. Then I began working my way through the logistics of preparing for a move to a foreign country. I had psychological and medical evaluations, got a passport, applied for a visa. . .and waited. And waited. And waited.

Many months passed with only an occasional phone call from the mission board to tell me they were still waiting for my visa. Then one day, they called to say that no more visas were being issued for

Pakistan, and none were expected to be issued in the near future. But they assured me that the "freeze" would eventually be lifted, and I would be on my way.

I began to wonder if God had really meant for me to go to Pakistan in the first place even though the circumstances that came together to bring me to this point could hardly have been coincidental. And life can be put on "hold" for just so long; then you have to get on with it. I did. I arranged to spend the summer of 1965 in Mexico with a friend and study Spanish there. I already had a passport and almost before I knew it, I had my plane ticket.

Just before the school year ended, a few days before I would be leaving for Mexico, another phone call came—this one from the mission board. My visa had been granted.

I should have been ecstatic. Instead, I was a bit miffed at God for pulling something like this on me. I had already rearranged my life, and Pakistan was no longer on my schedule. And my schedule was full.

But then I thought of Jonah. If you read the first chapter of Jonah in the Bible, you will know that God told Jonah to go to Nineveh to tell the people there about repentance. But Jonah had other plans, and Nineveh wasn't on *his* schedule either. Instead, he boarded a ship for Tarshish.

He never made it. Since he refused to go to Nineveh, God arranged for him to be thrown overboard where he was greeted by a resident whale. The whale promptly swallowed him and gave him less-than-luxurious room and board for three days. That should have been the end of Jonah, but God protected him just long enough for him to change his mind. After those three days the whale headed toward shore and upchucked (or whatever it is that whales do to get rid of a hapless meal)! The next thing Jonah knew, he was on land again and ready to do God's illogical bidding.

That reminder was all I needed. I knew that anything less than obedience to God's call would probably land me in the belly of a whale of a mess. Obedience was better. And unlike Jonah who was still snarling at God from Nineveh, I found my year serving my Lord in Pakistan one of the best in my life. As so often happens when you get involved in serving God by serving others, any aversion to the idea of servanthood quickly fades as names become faces, needs acquire hearts, and you discover that hands that help are often hands that heal. And many times those you serve discover the merits of service in the process and pass it on to others through their own loving acts.

Service Without Fanfare

Memorial Day has just come and gone, and throughout the day I witnessed many fitting memorials to the men and women who faithfully served our country. Flags were flying, flowers were placed respectfully on gravesites, paraders marched to patriotic music, and families gathered in memory of those who had died serving their country and in honor of those who had served and lived to tell about it.

My own celebration included a different kind of memorial in the form of service to a friend. I live in a part of the country where Memorial Day marks the beginning of the official planting season for flowers. My friend loves flowers; she has many flowerbeds around her house, and her home is ablaze with color by midsummer if flowers get planted on time. But this year, because of debilitating health problems she was unable to even think about planting flowers. So with a trunk full of garden tools and a backseat lined with food, another friend and I drove to our "mission field" for the day.

We planted geraniums, pulled weeds, served morning, noon, and evening meals, and honored the one who gave His life not just for His country but for the whole world. It was a special kind of Memorial Day in which we symbolically washed the feet of our ailing friend just as surely as if we were literally performing the ritual with our Lord in the Upper Room two thousand years ago.

Serving in Small Places

Opportunities to serve others come in many forms and show up in many places. But somehow we tend to look for them in the big things, often so big they overwhelm us, or seem out of reach, or require so much preplanning we give up before we get trapped into a commitment we wish we had not made. Realistically, most people will not go to another country to serve, or spearhead a major missions project with global connections, or even commit to a long-term assignment right in one's own hometown. The fact that we may not be able to serve in a big way, however, should not deter us from looking for opportunities to serve in small ways.

Take a friend of mine, for example, who every time she is in a doctor's office quietly prays for each person as they come in. Or whenever she hears a fire or ambulance siren prays for all the people involved, those needing assistance and those providing it. Or whenever she passes a school she prays for the students and staff and their families. And probably most intriguing of all, she regularly prays for all the people in the world who have no one to pray for them. Is that serving? I think so!

Another friend of mine is a great cook, and every time she sees a mouth to feed, a plate to fill, a pantry to stock, or someone whose spirits need lifting with a warm blueberry pie, she dons her apron and does food. I have a physician friend who sees patients from all over the world during the week, and then volunteers to help a neighbor move, mows the church lawn, or gives his wife a day out with her friends away from the kids on Saturdays. Are these people serving? Yes, indeed!

Others whose service is often taken for granted or overlooked altogether are Sunday school teachers, church nursery attendants, lay people who visit sick people, and sick people who inspire those of us who are well. The child with no forearms who fetches a drink for the one without legs, the school nurse who knows when a hug is more important than a Band-Aid, the child with gloves who gives one to a friend who has none, and then together they clutch each other's bare hand to stay warm.

Is this what Jesus meant when He said "I was an hungered, and ye gave me meat: I was thirsty, and ye gave me drink: I was a stranger, and ye took me in: Naked, and ye clothed me: I was sick, and ye visited me: I was in prison, and ye came unto me" (Matthew 25: 35–36)? I think so. In fact, it is impossible to meet Jesus at the cross, walk in His footsteps, and then fail to follow His example of serving others.

Sharing the Load

Serving others can be immensely gratifying, but with so many needs in the world and so many demands on one's time, how does one decide when to step forward and volunteer and when to pass? Sometimes an incident occurs abruptly and requires immediate assistance, leaving no time to consider the options.

On one such occasion, a physician friend of mine was riding a high-speed elevator from the ground floor of a tall building to the forty-second floor. The ride strained the eardrums of the adults aboard, but it literally took the breath away from one tiny baby clasped tightly in his mother's arms. By the time they reached the top, the baby was blue and not breathing. Without a thought about anything but saving a life, the doctor grabbed the baby and performed mouth-to-mouth resuscitation. Had he stopped to consider the possibility of malpractice litigation, or whether the baby might have a serious communicable disease, or whether his efforts might prove unsuccessful, he would surely have lost that opportunity to be of service. Instead, he saved a life.

Other times, a decision about serving does not need to be made so quickly, and pros and cons can be weighed. But always it is important to pray for God's guidance so one neither misses a divine opportunity to serve, nor commits to some service project God really intended for someone else.

Incline Your Ears

Many years ago, a minister friend of my family flew his private plane into a local airport and joined us as a houseguest. Over the next several days, I listened to many tales of the perils and pleasures of life at fifteen thousand feet. I trusted this godly man, but I wasn't sure I trusted him enough to view the world from fifteen thousand feet with him. One day, however, I found myself seated next to him in the cockpit of his plane—at fifteen thousand feet! As every familiar landmark below faded into an eerie blur, I was preoccupied with a single question: "How do you know if you get off course?"

His response relieved me. Clinging tightly to his head was a set of earphones through which he received a constant audible signal. This signal was keyed to the flight path that would get us safely to our destination. It was transmitted from the air traffic control station assigned to our flight, by the air traffic controller to whom my friend would be held accountable. As long as he was flying exactly on course, the sound in his ears was unmistakable. As soon as he began veering off course in any direction, that sound began to fade. When he brought the plane back into the proper flight path in response, the unmistakable sound returned.

I was struck with the realization that an untrustworthy and disreputable guide in that control tower could spell disaster for this trip. I was also struck with the confidence of my friend, the pilot, in the reliability of that signal. Another thing struck me. Those earphones never left his ears even while he was explaining to me how they worked. He remained constantly vigilant and responsive to that signal, and even when the landscape below was unfamiliar and unnerving, he *knew* we were on the right flight path.

What a comfort that was. But what greater comfort it is to know that we do not have to get a pilot's license and ascend to fifteen, twenty, or thirty-five thousand feet to don the earphones, tune into the control tower, and follow the guiding beep. It's really very simple. All we need to do is follow the wisdom in Proverbs 3:6: "In all thy ways acknowledge him, and he shall direct thy paths."

May I Serve You?

The Assignment

I wish there were an easy formula for distinguishing between serving and slavery, between obeying the Lord's call on the one hand and being held captive to needs you simply can't say "no" to on the other. That distinction is not easy, and too many people make it either after they have missed a priceless opportunity to serve, or they have hopelessly overcommitted themselves with no graceful way out.

The first step in making the distinction is to pray. Ask God to, in some way, communicate His will to you about a particular decision. Following that, here are a couple litmus tests:

> *Return to Psalm 100:2. If you can gladly commit yourself to a particular cause and cheerfully serve as you honor that commitment, that light is probably green. Second, if you have a sense of inner peace, or if you at least have an absence of inner turmoil and confusion about making the commitment, that light is also probably green.*

Should you make a wrong decision, never hesitate to go back and attempt to remake it. If that is not possible, learn a good lesson, fulfill your commitment in the best way you can and move on. God does not hold you to a standard of absolute perfection in making the right choices about service to Him. Nor should you hold yourself to such a standard if you discover you have missed the mark.

8

OBEY?
YOU MUST BE KIDDING!

For as by one man's disobedience
many were made sinners,
so by the obedience of one
shall many be made righteous.

ROMANS 5:19

When Adam disobediently took that first bite out of the apple in the Garden of Eden, the entire human race was handed a death sentence. When Jesus obediently bowed to the will of His Father, even to the point of dying on the cross, He commuted that death sentence for all who would ask. The difference between Jesus' obedience and Adam's disobedience is literally the difference between life and death. Not all acts of obedience are lifesaving, nor are all acts of disobedience deadly. But obedience is, by definition, a virtue, disobedience a vice. Jesus was the perfect model for obedience. But over time the concept of obedience has fallen into disrepute.

The word "obey" can be found sixty-nine times in the King James Version of the Bible; the word "obedience" twelve. That's a lot of divine sanction for a concept rarely heard above a whisper anymore, almost never seen in print, and seldom, if ever, included in even the most demanding treatises on behavior.

There are no substitutes for obedience. As outmoded and politically offensive as the notion of obedience has become, dispensing with it is a design for disaster, and the price of disobedience, while sometimes not immediate, is often very high. If you would like to know just how high, let me tell you a little story.

Too Little and Too Late!

Once upon a time, several thousand years ago, God got sick and tired of the fact that almost all the people He had created on earth were bad—I mean *really* bad. There was only one family in the whole world who remained faithful to Him, so He devised a plan whereby He would save that family, destroy the unfaithful, and essentially start the human race all over.

No, this is not a fairy tale; this really happened. And the family is that of Noah. Out of the blue one day, God told Noah that He was going to send a great flood that would cover the whole earth and destroy everyone except those in a specially built ark. And while Noah had never seen an ark, nor had he ever heard of one, God told him to build one. He even gave Noah exact instructions for how to build it.

The picture gets even crazier! Since the beginning of time, not one drop of rain had ever fallen. How in the world could there be such an illogical event as a flood? But Noah didn't ask questions; he just obediently set about to build an ark.

His neighbors jeered. His carpenter colleagues ridiculed him and refused to help. His suppliers wouldn't deliver necessary building materials so he made his own—from scratch. He took this nonsense for over a hundred years and just kept working, building that ark. Finally one day the ark was finished, and God instructed him to take a pair of every living thing on earth and put them on board.

Try to imagine, if you can, how utterly hare-brained Noah was beginning to look. The sky was cloudless, the ground was dry, the ark was a monstrous eyesore in the middle of nowhere. Two of each of thousands of animal species went marching or crawling or flying through its gaping door, and Noah, his wife, his three sons, and their wives, only eight people in all, obediently boarded.

I believe, however, that the ark was large enough to accommodate every man, woman, and child on earth at that time, had they wanted to get on. But no one else did. So ignoring the relentless, raucous derision of curious and amused bystanders, only eight people boldly walked up that plank, just before God shut and sealed the door. Even after the door was shut, the crowds that had gathered outside continued their heckling.

But obedience has its rewards, and disobedience eventually exacts a heavy toll. It didn't take long for both to become evident. Just a little rain, then a little more rain. At first, those outside the ark were ecstatic and refreshed and encouraged by the much-needed rain. But suddenly, the clouds began looking ominous, and the rain came in torrents; clearly, something cataclysmic was about to happen. Then that word "flood" began to register.

"*Flood!* Oh no!"

Could Noah have been right all along? Were they on the outside the harebrained foolish ones? Then it occurred to them that maybe they could still book passage on Noah's belittled monstrosity, just in case. At least they stopped jeering and heckling and started crying and pleading and banging on the door. But it was too late. The door was shut! God kept His promise and flooded the entire earth. Noah and his seven family members reaped their reward for obedience, and lived. And everyone else, absolutely everyone, paid the ultimate price of disobedience: They all died.

The Moral

There's a moral here. When you sense that God is telling you to do something, don't quibble with Him, just do it. Equally important, if you suspect He is trying to stop you from doing something, often in the form of giving you an eerie disquiet about it, stop in your tracks.

But let me give you a caution about this. If you have not taken that life-changing, humbling walk to the cross, and you have not surrendered your life to the will of Jesus who died there for you, and you are not tuned into His control tower, the only totally trustworthy control tower in the world, you cannot count on the accuracy of the signals you are hearing. There is only one other such tower, and the man in charge of that is a damned, deviant scoundrel. Call him what you will, but his real title is the devil, and he would like nothing better than for you to listen to his twisted cues and land in the middle of the same dark and desperate and eternally wretched kingdom in which he resides. Misery after all, loves company.

But then, happiness also loves company. And when you listen to the signals in God's control tower, in the end you'll find eternal happiness and joy.

Obey? You Must Be Kidding!

Obedience in Eilat

We were midway through our ten-day tour of Israel, and most of us were tired. We awoke to a beautiful, bright, sunny day in Eilat, a charming resort city on the Gulf of Aqaba in Israel. This was a day and a place put into our tour itinerary for recreation and relaxation. Eilat was just the right place for both, and we were given a number of attractive options for touring this beautiful city and its coastal charm.

I sensed, however, that this was not a day for me to join a tour or catch a ride into one of the chic shopping areas of Eilat. God had another plan for me that day, and while I had no idea what the details of the plan were, I had no question that God and I had some important business to attend to.

My roommate for this tour was the tour coordinator, and she had been sick and getting sicker during most of the tour so far. The evening before, though barely able, she and I had gone on foot to scout around the city for a drug store where she might get some nonprescription medication that would help her get well. We found one where we also found a very compassionate pharmacist who gave her some medications he thought would help.

By morning, however, she had become even sicker. I knew she needed medical help, but finding a doctor in a foreign country requires an act of God. I didn't realize finding that pharmacist again, by myself this time, would also require God's help. But I somehow knew if I could get back to him, he could help. So without a clue about the name of the pharmacy, the name of the pharmacist or the address, or even what general direction to go, I started out.

Now I have to tell you something about myself. My sense of direction is not trustworthy, maybe because attention to detail is not my forte. I get lost easily, sometimes even in familiar territory, and nothing in the scenery here looked even remotely familiar. Before long I realized I was lost.

I stopped someone to ask for directions. That wasn't an easy task because I didn't know where I was going. Armed with some vague but kind advice, I started out again. Soon I was again hopelessly disoriented and had no idea even how to return to our hotel. In fact, I had not even paid close attention to the name of the hotel in which we were staying.

I decided the time had come for a real heart-to-heart with God. Along the sidewalk was a cement bench so I stopped, bowed my head, and prayed. Did I ever pray! I knew God knew where I was even though I didn't. He also knew the location of that pharmacy and how to get me there. But what if the same pharmacist were not on duty this day, and what if he could give my friend nothing more without a doctor's prescription, and what if he didn't remember me? And what if he wouldn't. . . Well, I finally just let go of all the questions and asked God for a miracle.

From that moment, I moved out of the driver's seat of this little venture and asked God to take charge. . .and I walked. . .and walked. . .and walked. Then I decided to cross the street, not knowing why. Suddenly I began recognizing buildings and streets and landmarks from the night before. Just as suddenly, I found that little drug store. When I entered, the same pharmacist was behind the counter, and though he did not say so, he seemed to be expecting me.

I painted him the grim word picture of my sick friend and pled for something more to give her. As if following the script of a screenplay, he opened a drawer, withdrew a package, and said, "I am not supposed to do this, but this will help her." In the package was a powerful antibiotic available only by prescription. I am still marveling today about how that package got into that drawer, but I didn't ask any questions. He handed me the package; I thanked him and was off.

Without a single misstep, I found our hotel. My friend started immediately on the medication, and within twelve hours its effects were evident, and we had our tour coordinator back. As the rest of our tour group recounted stories from their varied explorations of Eilat that day, my story was no match. My day was not one of shopping or sightseeing. It was a day of blind obedience to my Lord—a day in which I learned that obedience does have its rewards.

Trust and Obey: A Word of Caution

An old hymn entitled "Trust and Obey" captures an essential component of obedience—trust—without which submitting to the authority of someone can be rather risky. Not everyone is trustworthy, and obedience to someone who is not can blow an irreparable hole into a perfectly legitimate and noble act.

Spouses must be trusted for marriages to work. Parents must be trusted for families to function. Pastors must be trusted for churches to thrive. Health care providers must be trusted for treatment plans to be followed. Educators must be trusted for students to learn. Rarely does a day go by when we are not duty-bound to trust someone enough to obey them; otherwise, much of life would break down.

Unfortunately, not everyone is trustworthy. Even more unfortunately, that includes some pastors and preachers.

The story is told of a group of people who were meeting to discuss reasons why Christianity lacked integrity and why Christians are sometimes untrustworthy. The subject seemed to hit a nerve because over a thousand people showed up. One after the other, people rose to poke holes in the trustworthiness of pastors, expose hypocrites in pews, castigate Christian businessmen who engage in dubious business practices, even highlight the tragedy of Christian parents who abuse their children.

When all the points of view had been aired, the

moderator summarized the whole sordid list and then said, "But you have not said one word against Jesus."

No wonder. Jesus is the standard-bearer for Christianity, the One about whom the hymn "Trust and Obey" was written. He is the One to keep your eyes on, the One to trust confidently, the One to obey absolutely. Everyone else, sooner or later, will disappoint you simply because everyone else, Christians included, is human.

The Blessings of Obedience

Despite the risks, obedience does have its rewards. It also works best if we understand a biblical "pecking order" within which the blessings of obedience are likely to flourish. Not surprisingly, that order of rank is best taught and played out in the home.

"Both the Old and New Testaments agree that children have only one responsibility in the family— to obey their parents," writes John C. Hagee, editor of *Prophecy Study Bible*. If you have any question about that, read Proverbs 1:8 and Ephesians 6:1-3. Every other responsibility of a child follows, like tumbling dominoes, from that initial submission to parental authority.

And from where do parents get their authority? A divinely ordained hierarchy structures the entire family: Husbands are in submission to God, wives are also in submission to God under the leadership of their husbands (who are in submission to God), and children are in submission to their parents (who are in submission to God). If you have any question about that, read Ephesians 5.

Submitting obediently to a higher authority, however, is not an innate characteristic. It must be learned, and God assigned the primary task of teaching it to parents. If parents are not themselves submitted to the authority of Almighty God, this entire divinely commissioned chain of command is seriously weakened, and the whole matter of being obedient can become a well-intentioned nightmare. On the other hand, if everyone in this chain of submission is dutifully submitted, life is remarkably livable and everyone benefits.

It is no statistical fluke that the rise in violated trust by adults, as well as the brazen disobedience of children, has paralleled the tragic disintegration of the family. Unless one has learned to be obedient in the hallowed halls of home under the loving guidance of trustworthy parents, nothing short of a miracle will fill in those blanks. If achieving smoothly running harmonious families were the only reason to live and teach obedience, that would be reason enough. But there is more, much more, to it than that.

The Ultimate Obedience

As difficult as obedience may be at times, and as much as one may question the merits of obedience, there is an ultimate payoff. Only one route leads to heaven, and we all, kings and servants alike, obtain our ticket the same humble way—on our knees in obedient submission to the king of kings. Such obedience has only rewards: immediate, long term, and eternal.

The Assignment

Be obedient, first of all to God. Then identify your place in His hierarchy, and no matter where that place is, like it or not, obedience to someone will be in the picture somewhere. Be obedient. If, in addition to *being* obedient, you are responsible for *teaching* obedience, your assignment is even more awesome.

9

LOVE WHO?

A new commandment I give unto you,
That ye love one another;
as I have loved you,
that ye also love one another.

JOHN 13:34

One of the most common themes in the Bible is love. One of the most frequent expressions of that theme is the command to love. It is easy to miss the fact that Jesus tells us twice in this verse, John 13:34, to love. He even tells us to model our love after His own. That is a really tough standard because His love for us cost Him His life. There is no greater love than that!

Someone Who Knows

On April 14, 1912, John Harper was on his way to preach at Chicago's Moody Memorial Church. Days earlier, a friend of his, John English, pled with him to postpone his trip and even offered to pay his ticket for a later voyage. English had prayed about Harper's passage on the *Titanic,* and he had an ominous sense of doom about this maiden voyage on the ship that "Not even God could sink." But Harper was on a mission for God, and he was not deterred by his friend's warning.

At 11:40 P.M. on this memorable night, the *Titanic* and an iceberg vied for the same space in the vast Atlantic; the iceberg won. Both heroes and villains were on board that night, and the jolt of the icy battle thrust both into action. Villains have a way of telling their own story, and history books have already aptly recorded some of the more ignoble of their deeds during the two and one-half hours that followed the impact. But heroes often get lost in the silence of anonymity, and were it not for Moody Adams' riveting book, *The Titanic's Last Hero*, we would probably never have heard of John Harper.

The night before the collision, while others were partying, Harper was seen on the ship's deck guiding a young man on that trek to the cross. When disaster struck, there were not enough life jackets for everyone on board; Harper gave his to someone who had none. Once the full import of the ship's damage began to dawn, and as fellow passengers screamed in futile desperation, Harper comforted panicked passengers with calm, the calm that comes from knowing that the Lord Jesus Christ saves. Harper was heard calling out over and over that message of hope to desperate passengers. And in a final act of heroism, a man clinging to a board in the icy Atlantic drifted close enough to Harper to hear him call out one last time before going down himself, "Are you saved?" The man shot back "No!" Then Harper threw him the only life line he would ever need. He shouted "Believe on the Lord Jesus Christ and thou shalt be saved!" The man clinging to that piece of wood later testified in Hamilton, Ontario, that he was "John Harper's last convert."

"Greater love hath no man than this, that a man lay down his life for his friends" (John 15:13). John Harper knew that "greater love" and even more. I am sure most of those people he gave his life for that night, he did not know as friends. Still, he laid down his life for them.

Love Thy Neighbor

It is one thing to love a friend. But love our neighbor? I don't think so! Paul instructs us in Galatians 5:14, "Thou shalt love thy neighbour as thyself." Surely, however, Paul never had anyone living next door who played their tasteless music too loud, who constantly took shortcuts through his groomed lawn, who borrowed his tools without returning them, or who always had problems but never solutions. Maybe he wasn't talking about people like that. Or was he?

A lawyer once asked Jesus the same question. The lawyer, hoping to exclude "the undesirables" in his life from the definition, asked, "Who is my neighbour?" (Luke 10:29). Jesus answered with this story:

A man going from Jerusalem to Jericho was stopped, robbed, and wounded by thugs who left him for dead. Three strangers passed him, all three noting his predicament. The first two crossed the road and went on. The third, a Samaritan, stopped, administered first aid, lifted the injured man onto his donkey, transported him to an inn, and arranged for his medical care. Not only that, the Samaritan stayed in touch with the injured man and the innkeeper in case more help was needed.

Then Jesus asked the lawyer to answer a question: "Who was the good neighbour?" This was a multiple-choice test, but only one answer was possible, and the lawyer got it right: "He who showed mercy on him."

There is something almost childlike about the good Samaritan, and sometimes children seem to get the point of this parable more easily and readily than adults.

Little Samaritans

I watch for a certain little boy every Sunday morning because he is so unusually sensitive and loving—and only four years old. His parents are divorced, but they are both unusually loving parents. I also watch for a lady, many decades older than the little boy. She lives in a wheelchair where she has spent most of her life. She was born with spina bifida, and her body is a wreck on the outside, but inside she's a raving beauty. Together, these two make the most unlikely couple, but every Sunday they somehow seem to find each other. The little boy parks himself by her large wheel, touches her hand, and reaches for a hug. She makes sure he is protected from the wheel, sandwiches his little hand between hers, and then wraps her arms around him. I have been searching for a name for this little routine, and I think I have found one: It is called "love."

Then there was another little boy, this one autistic. He is quite a handsome gentleman now, but I remember him as a kindergartner. He seemed always to be doing or saying something so offbeat and outlandish that his classmates, even at that early age, were wary of befriending him. He was a loner but not the usual kind. *He* had no friends, but he was a friend to everyone.

Every time one of his classmates was disciplined and had to be separated in some way from the rest of the class, this little boy would drop whatever he was doing and join the transgressor. He would stand beside him in the corner or sit next to him on the floor beside the teacher and always looked with painful sympathy directly into the chastised child's eyes. Many times I observed this when I visited the classroom. And as hard as the teacher tried to break him of this little exercise in compassion, he never gave up. Invariably he would himself become the object of discipline because of this behavior and would be sent back to his seat with a reprimand. But as soon as the spotlight shifted, he would take off again to complete his aborted mission. I think his teacher called this disobedience. I called it love.

Marriage: The Prototype for Love

Love comes in many packages. None is more beautiful than that shared in a healthy, joyous, secure marriage. It is no coincidence that God has chosen to portray our relationship with Him in the language of marriage. There are many parallels.

Marriage is first of all a relationship. Jesus, outside of a relationship, is merely a topic of conversation, a name without a face, even a curiosity. Marriage is bonded in love. A relationship with Jesus is also bonded in love, the love which God showed when "He gave [us] His only begotten Son," so that believing on Him, we will "not perish, but have everlasting life" (John 3:16). Marriage is meant to be permanent. Once we accept God's gift of His Son, we are part of the family of God for life. Marriage is hard work; to keep it alive you have to tend it like a garden, spend time with your spouse, do everything you can to please him or her, and keep communicating. To keep our relationship with Jesus alive we must tend to His work as if it were a garden, spend time with Him, do everything we know to please Him, and keep praying to Him.

Relationships are never perfect, because humans are not perfect. Marriages can, however, withstand an onslaught of imperfections, provided they are bathed in the warmth of unconditional, loyal, tender love, the kind defined in 1 Corinthians 13. So, too, can our relationship with Jesus stand up to a host of imperfections. But in this relationship, we are the only ones who are imperfect. Jesus is absolute perfection, and only as we bathe our relationship in His perfect love does our bond with Him become permanent.

Love Who?

Putting a Face on Love

Back in the late 1950s, I watched as one of my best friends, a nursing classmate, fell head over heels in love with one of her best friends. We both knew this was shaping up to be a love affair designed in heaven.

Every time this suitor sent my friend anything requiring his signature, no matter how seemingly insignificant, he prefaced it with these poignant words, "All my love forever." I often wondered if he really considered the full meaning of that phrase—and if he really was presenting his love over and over as a lifetime gift to her. Now, forty years later, I have the answer.

Two years ago, this friend of mine returned home from a doctor's appointment to a message on her answering machine asking her to call her doctor as soon as possible. Thus began a raging ordeal with a large, albeit benign, tumor hopelessly entwined with vital parts of her brain. Today, five surgeries, thousands of dollars, extensive, strenuous, medical travel, a tattered body, a blurry mind, and many shattered dreams later, these two people are still madly, head over heels in love with each other. How have they done it?

They have not done everything right. In fact, theirs has been far from a perfect marriage. But when they faltered, love was the glue which held them together.

Our relationship with Jesus does not require perfection either; it requires love. And God *is* love (1 John 4:8) When we falter, His love gathers our pieces and glues them together.

One cannot really love without knowing God. And one cannot know God without having a relationship with His Son, Jesus. And one cannot have a relationship with Jesus without loving one another as He has loved us.

Love in Action

One Christmastime, I was visiting friends in Rawalpindi, Pakistan. These friends lived in the staff house of a hospital dedicated exclusively to the treatment of people with leprosy.

I am a registered nurse, but leprosy was a dreaded condition I had only read about in the Bible and medical texts and seen gruesomely portrayed in movies. If anyone had ever told me I would some day look leprosy in the face and do a major overhaul of my hands-off attitude toward "lepers," I would have quickly set them straight.

But this was the day. I was sitting at a table looking out the kitchen window when I saw a man preparing a bucket of warm melted wax out on the lawn. Aha! It was Christmas, and this must be a candle-making project, I thought. Just then, another man walked up to the bucket and extended his hands to the first man, who reached out and took hold of them. I noticed then several fingers missing from those outstretched hands and numerous white patches mottling his otherwise dark skin. Goose bumps rose on my skin as I realized what I was witnessing.

Gently and tenderly those grasped hands were lowered into the bucket until melted wax covered them beyond the wrist. The wax quickly dried and the warmth from it stimulated the blood flow to cells struggling to stay alive in a battle with leprosy. Then, just short of a skin burn, the wax was peeled off as gently and tenderly as it had been applied. The two men exchanged a hug and a smile, both beaming with love and hope.

The scene was repeated over and over as patient

after patient stepped forward, not just for wax therapy, but for a touch of love, a real live warm touch of love. I later found out that patients with leprosy came to this special hospital from many parts of the globe, but not just to have warm wax applied to their affected extremities. Leprous fingers and toes can be bathed in warm wax anywhere in the world. But getting wrapped in a hug in the process transcends the boundaries of medical practice and reaches into souls also struggling to stay alive.

These souls had come here not only to be treated for their leprosy. They came here in search of love—and they found it!

The Assignment

If you have not yet fallen in love with God's Son, there is no better time than now to begin that romance. And if you would like the perfect blueprint for love, read 1 Corinthians 13. Then begin obeying that "new commandment" in John 13:34 and "love one another."

10

HELPFUL KINDNESS

Be ye kind one to another, tenderhearted . . .
EPHESIANS 4:32

The story is told of a man who had just moved into a town when he stopped by the grocery store to pick up some food. He asked the grocer what kind of neighbors lived in that community. The grocer asked him, "What kind of neighbors did you have where you came from?"

The man replied, "Mean, never saw such mean people."

The grocer nodded. "You will find them mean here, too."

The next day the man's wife came into the store and asked the grocer the same question. When the grocer repeated his query, the man's wife replied, "Why, they were the finest people you ever saw."

The grocer answered, "Well, Lady, you will find these people the finest, kindest neighbors you ever saw, too."

While kindness tends to breed kindness, unkindness often reproduces itself, too. But when the apostle Paul instructs us in Ephesians 4:32 to be kind to one another, he leaves no room whatsoever for unkindness, no matter how mean or unkind someone may be to us. Being nice to someone who is nice to you is easy. It takes a touch of divine grace to return good for evil.

Many years ago, a professor by the name of John Kant decided to visit his native country of Silesia in southwest Poland. As he was traveling on horseback through the forests to reach his destination, he was overtaken by robbers. They stripped him of everything but his clothes. They even took his horse and then asked if he had anything more. He replied, "Nothing," and was permitted to go on.

Far down the road and out of sight of the robbers,

he felt something hard in the hem of his coat. He suddenly remembered he had sewn some gold coins into the hem. Just as suddenly, he found himself surrounded again by the same robbers, as if they were checking up on his truthfulness.

Without even considering the consequences, he told them meekly, "I have told you something which was untrue, but it was not intentional." He then showed them the place in his hem where the gold coins were hidden. No one made a move to take them.

He was astonished as one by one the men walked up to him to return first his wallet, then his Bible; then one man returned even his horse and helped him remount. He thanked them for their kindness and rode safely away, having overcome evil with good.

This true story could have had a very different and tragic ending, but Professor Kant's behavior was not determined by some preconceived outcome. He was not only an honest man, he was a kind man, too. After all, he acquired his working definition of kindness in that Bible the robbers had stolen and then returned.

The Triumph of Tough Kindness

Several years ago, the phone rang late one evening in the home of some dear friends. It was their daughter, a senior in a collegiate nursing program. She was about to graduate. In fact, graduation was close enough that they were already making plans for the trip to share in the celebration.

But something had gone terribly wrong; they knew that by the emotion in her voice. Grades had just been posted, and their daughter had failed the final exam in one of the most important courses of her entire program. The anticipated graduation was out of the question and out of reach. The picture, in fact, was sufficiently bleak that it challenged the wisdom of any other recourse but having her pack up, cave in, and come home. Now this was pain—plural pain!

The natural inclination when one is in pain is to seek relief. Relief was available. It would have been a simple matter to welcome her back to the comforts of home, resume the role of protective parenting, and in this case, financially bail her out of this whole troublesome affair.

There was also the possibility of exerting some weighty influence in the situation. After all, one could have argued the injustice of permitting a single, unrepresentative event to delete a whole program and crash a career. But these parents did none of the above.

Over the summer, they shared many tears with their daughter, held her hand, kissed her wounds, hurt passionately for her, and cheered her on. This was not the end of the world, and while they were ready to support her in whatever choice she made, they strongly suggested only one.

This was a particularly difficult dilemma because the failed course was not scheduled to be offered again until the second half of the following year. But when life delivers you a shipment of lemons, you juice them and sweeten them and prepare an exotic beverage of some sort. They began gently walking their daughter back into the kitchen to concoct a recipe for recovery.

One year and many more tears later, she graduated. The timing of her graduation put her in exact alignment to land a plum position at a well-regarded hospital in one of the most desirable cities in the country in which to live and work. It also coincided with the arrival in that city of a young physician who was later to become her husband. Today they are the parents of two fine sons who are the newest beneficiaries of the idea that standing back is sometimes more kind than stepping in.

Spontaneous Kindness: Little Time to Think

Sometimes an act of kindness can expose one to risks that must be weighed against the calculated benefits. If an act of kindness can put you in a dangerous or compromising position, be especially sure God has assigned you to that mission. Often there is little time to decide.

One morning in the fall of 1995, while visiting a friend in Turkey, I set out alone, on foot, to explore the sights and sounds and sensations of Ankara. To reach the heart of the city, I had to walk up a steep hill, along a smoothly paved road, past many houses and a few other pedestrians. I soon overtook a heavy-set, well-dressed lady, also on her way up the hill, who was stopping frequently to rest and catch her breath. I paid little attention as I passed her, even though

I sensed something was wrong.

I had learned many years before that every culture has its protocols, and a breach of them, even innocently or with noble intent, can create some sticky problems. Just the day before, I had gone out on the balcony of my friend's apartment to photograph what I thought were benign street scenes. It wasn't long before I was nearly required to surrender my camera to some vigilant, resolute policemen. They were guarding the privacy and security of an anonymous government official living across the street, and a camera lens pointed in that direction understandably aroused their suspicions. I didn't want to risk repeating an innocent transgression so soon.

When I reached the top of the hill, I looked back at the lady and immediately knew this was no time to calculate risk. I hurried back down to her, asked if she needed help, and gestured for her to take my arm.

I spoke to her in English, and she replied in Turkish. After all, this was her country, and it was I who needed to figure out some way to communicate. I had purchased a Turkish pocket dictionary for just such occasions as this and then neglected to pack it. But there is a language that emanates from the heart, and we both seemed to have some reasonable command of that.

With no hesitation, she took my arm and gestured to her heart, indicating she was in some kind of distress. Together, we very slowly made it up the hill, neither of us understanding one word of our conversation. Neither of us cared. These were moments to savor. Even after we reached the top, we continued on together until our separate itineraries parted us. I crossed the street, then looked back to catch one final glimpse of this unusual companion. In a contemporary rendition of a song from the past, "I was looking back at her as she was looking back at me," and we both waved a thank you, unmistakable in any language.

The Heart of the Matter

There are times when we must decide among a number of possible courses of action, all of which could be considered acts of kindness, but only one of which is the one God had in mind. Not that the others would be wrong, but you can sometimes misjudge a situation and then have to clean up an unnecessarily messy act of kindness.

I have become a master at such cleanups, but let me tell you a story in which the heart of kindness lay in compromise.

Several years ago, I was counseling an elementary school student whose standard everyday behavior was incorrigible. In the opinion of many, he didn't belong in a public school, and I became his apologist, even for essentially harmless behaviors normally not requiring a defense. His occasional moments of civility were blurred by a reputation befitting a villain and thus were usually overlooked. They were often too brief to catch or too marginal to warrant giving him a break because of them. He had already spent so much time in the principal's office, he thought the principal was his private tutor.

I don't often write contracts in counseling, but this little guy needed his wings glued down, and a contract was one way to do that. The contract was simple; "Do what the teacher tells you to do the first time she tells you to do it." A trip to the principal's office meant a call to his parents and an unscheduled trip home. His parents were as fed up with his shenanigans as was nearly every other adult in his life and sometimes "fed up" can lead to some pretty disastrous consequences. He had already suffered some unusually severe punishments at home for lesser "crimes" than this and all of us hoped that fateful call would *never* need to be made.

Were we naive! I returned to my office one day to find a trembling little body occupying what was normally a very comforting chair. For many months, this little body and I had worked together to carve a success story out of a relentless barrage of failures. Even the naysayers had to admit it was paying off. Then this!

I fired off a few questions, and soon two of us were trembling. He had not simply blown the contract; he had exploded it. He was petrified; I was crushed. My head told me that a contract must be honored; my heart did not agree. Both he and I knew that a call home announcing this latest bombshell could be disastrous.

I cared deeply about this boy, and I could see no benefit in preserving a principle while destroying a tender soul. Besides, at that moment I recalled a conversation I overheard him having with his sister a few days earlier in which she asked him, "Is that lady always that kind to you?"

He replied, "She was born kind." He was counting on me now to be kind to him.

That meant I not only had a principle to honor, I had a reputation to preserve. Believe me, God and I had a quick and quiet conversation before I made my next move.

I called him close to my desk and with a spontaneous mix of sternness and compassion told him I was going to the principal's office myself to try and negotiate something. No further discussion was necessary.

The collective shared emotions that followed would have warmed a glacier. The principal, already fed up to his eyeballs with previous transgressions, knew instinctively this was an occasion for compromise. I was touched, not so much by the principal's unlikely concession, but by our singular sense that this compromised version of "help" would be more helpful than our usual adherence to "the letter of the law."

I returned to my office to deliver the verdict. The wait had taken its toll on my little friend, and he was white as a sheet. The whole episode had taken a toll on me, also, and I sat down at my desk and promptly sobbed. This was a moment of redemption, and the cost of it was one we were sharing.

In preparation for writing this chapter, I decided to track down this "little guy" and find out just how kind I had actually been to him that day. After many months of fruitless searching, I finally unraveled a chain of tangled leads and found a six-foot, two-inch young man who, years earlier, would not have come within ten feet of a hug. This day, after a breakfast of bacon and eggs and a heartwarming conversation laced with laughter and tears, we hugged. My mind flashed back to the scene in my office that day many years before. I was so thankful we broke that contract.

Overzealous Kindness

Sometimes sincere acts of kindness can produce results that by any definition are not kind at all. When that happens one must correct the situation if possible, learn a good lesson, and move on. But before even performing such an act, it is *always* a good idea to check in with God about what actually constitutes kindness in any particular situation. One of the best examples I know of kindness gone awry is one in nature.

This story has been restated in many variations over the years, but several years ago, while attending a seminar on early childhood development at the Gesell Institute in New Haven, Connecticut, I received a copy of this original version from *Zorba the Greek* by Kazantzakis:

> *I remembered one morning when I discovered a cocoon in the bark of a tree, just as a butterfly was making a hole in its case and preparing to come out. I waited a while, but it was too long appearing, and I was impatient. I bent over it and breathed on it to warm it. I warmed it as quickly as I could, and the miracle began to happen before my eyes, faster than life. The case opened, the butterfly started slowly crawling out, and I shall never forget my horror when I saw how its wings were folded back and crumpled; the wretched butterfly tried with its whole trembling body to unfold them. Bending over it, I tried to help*

*it with my breath. In vain. It needed to be
hatched out patiently, and the unfolding of the
wings should be a gradual process in the sun.
Now it was too late. My breath had forced the
butterfly to appear, all crumpled, before its
time. It struggled desperately and, a few seconds later, died in the palm of my hand.*

The natural inclination when observing someone
struggle is to get into the act and "help out." Unques-
tionably, many lives have been saved and hearts warmed
in response to this natural tendency. But "help" isn't
always helpful, and "kindness" isn't always kind.

Sometimes the greatest kindness one can offer in
a struggle is loving restraint.

The Other Side of Being Kind

On December 3, 1995, I arrived late in the evening
at Frankfurt Airport on a flight from Ankara, Turkey.
I had a thirteen-hour wait for my departure back to
the United States.

I had been away from home for about three

weeks, and my father, who was very ill when I left, had grown steadily worse. I was eager to get back to him, and the idea of being grounded in an airport for thirteen hours was a bitter pill to swallow.

I had just spent ten of the most exhilarating days of my life touring Israel and walking through the pages of my Bible in a way that reading through them never quite matched. The remainder of the three weeks I spent with a friend and colleague in Turkey, another spot on a Bible map that assumes a heartbeat as one walks in the footsteps of the apostle Paul.

About forty-eight hours earlier I had talked with my dad from my hotel in Cappadocia, Turkey, a biblical location he would normally have been bubbling to hear about. But his voice was weak, and the bubbles were gone. I needed to get home.

Now I was stuck at Frankfurt Airport which also seemed to eerily lose its bubbles around midnight that night: The lights were dimmed, the heat was lowered, concession stands were closed, people had disappeared. I read, paced, prayed, and visited and revisited every restroom in the airport—just because they were the only places with bright lights. They were also the only places I could find water, which, with a little creativity, I managed occasionally to dribble into my dry mouth. I was dying of thirst, and not a drinking fountain was in the place.

Before the shutdown, I was advised by one of the uniformed employees to go out and buy a bottle of water if I needed it badly enough. I thought he was kidding! I discovered, too late, that he wasn't. To buy a bottle of water at this late hour would have required exiting the main airport beyond the security gates, only to have to come back through them again.

The first leg of this trip had been to Israel with a tour group from Midnight Call Ministries. I had been through many international airports over the years, including this very one several years earlier. But I had never been through such tight security procedures as I was subjected to here this time. Had I been "profiled" as a suspicious traveler, I would have understood the depth of their invasion of my privacy and dignity. But all passengers were subjected to the same routine, and I especially did not want to have to go through the security gates again, at least not on this dreadful night.

I was tired. But sleep eluded me. While the available lounge chairs were exceptionally comfortable, I was exceptionally not. I was cold, but even more tormenting, I was rapidly absorbing the depressed mood of the setting. I was concerned about my father, even though before I left him, he and I had discussed the possibility that our next meeting could be in heaven. It sounded good, but I wasn't ready for that.

Somewhere smack in the middle of the night, when I had just about run out of coping mechanisms, I heard sounds I would normally have ignored. Considering the predicament I was in, those sounds rang like a bell choir, even though they actually came from a custodial cart rolling up the hall. I was overjoyed when I realized a real live person was attached to it. I hadn't seen a real live anything in hours.

Apparently I looked pathetic. When this dear cleaning lady saw me, without any hesitation, she took two large garbage bags from her cart, brought them over to me, and motioned for me to cover up. I knew little German beyond "danke," but nothing more was necessary. She gracefully acknowledged my thanks, returned to her cart, and went on her way. I never saw her again.

I immediately unfolded the cold stiff plastic bags and covered myself. They not only warmed me, they gave me a much-needed sense of security and comfort, enough so that I soon fell asleep. When I awakened a few hours later, the normal airport bustle was in full swing. I looked through the airport for that special lady whose lowly act of kindness I wanted to acknowledge again. I couldn't find her, nor could I find anyone who could even remotely connect with my story of someone coming by in the middle of the night with a custodial cart. I gave up the search when I heard my flight being called for boarding.

With those two blue plastic garbage bags tucked safely in my carry-on bag, I got on the plane and headed for New York. Upon arriving at JFK Airport, and with one more leg of my journey still to go, I called home. For thirteen hours I had sat in an airport in Germany next to a wall of payphones without ever thinking I should call home and check on my dad. Now I learned he had died a little after midnight, which in German time, coincided with the appearance of one special nameless lady whose kindness helped get me through one of the worst nights of my life.

It was a lesson in kindness I will never forget.

Someone once said, "Wherever there is a human

being, there is an opportunity for kindness." And wherever there is an opportunity for kindness, there is always that possibility that someone might miss the opportunity, or reject it, or even yield to the temptation to be unkind. Did you ever wonder what the world would be like if everyone were kind?

History May Be Born in an Act of Kindness

One day, as a poor Scottish farmer named Fleming was working on his farm, he heard a cry for help from a nearby swamp. He responded and found a terrified boy, mired to his waist in muck, struggling to free himself. Fleming rescued him from what could have been a slow and frightful death.

The next day a fancy carriage pulled up in front of his very unfancy home. An elegantly dressed nobleman descended and introduced himself as the father of the rescued lad. He came to repay the farmer for his selfless act of kindness in saving his son. The farmer declined, indicating he could not accept payment for his deed.

Just then, the farmer's son appeared at the door of

their little shack. The nobleman asked if that was the farmer's son.

"Yes," the farmer replied with pride.

The nobleman then asked the farmer if he could make a deal with him. "Let me take him and give him a good education. If he is anything like his dad, he'll grow up to be a man you can be proud of."

Fleming accepted the offer. Years passed and eventually his son graduated from St. Mary's Hospital Medical School in London. That distinguished graduate turned out to be Sir Alexander Fleming, the man who discovered penicillin.

Years later, the nobleman's son contracted pneumonia. His life was again spared, this time because of penicillin. And the course of history was forever changed. The nobleman? Lord Randolph Churchill. His son? Sir Winston!

The Assignment

"Be ye kind one to another, tenderhearted . . ."
EPHESIANS 4:32

11

FORGIVE? YES.
FORGET? HMMM. . .

But if ye forgive men their trespasses,
your heavenly Father will also forgive you.
MATTHEW 6:14

I was standing beside my father's casket as hundreds of people filed by to pay their respects. A few hours earlier, I had gotten off the plane in Syracuse, New York, feeling as if I had a rope twisted around my aching heart. I was so much looking forward to seeing my dad again and sharing my Holy Land experiences with him. He was an avid defender of Israel and would have loved to visit there, but I got to go instead. Now he had died before I returned, and he wouldn't even be able to relive the experience with me. Among a rash of heavy feelings I had that day, I was working very hard not to feel guilty for having left him when he was so ill.

As I was struggling with those feelings between hugs and handshakes, I looked to the back of the sanctuary where lines of people kept streaming in. Then I spotted her.

Months earlier I had found myself in the middle of disputing parties, trying to mediate a fiery truce. In the heat of it, I personally became the focus of attack and was hurled an accusation I couldn't believe I was hearing. I had always thought I would rather die than be accused of such a thing. But now, here I was, being accused of just such a thing, and I could see God wasn't going to let me die my way out of it.

Since I was the mediator and my own character was not even supposed to be the issue, I did a quick mend and pulled the discussion back to the truce. But I was hurting. All day I was hurting. And before that day was finished, I was feeling much more than hurt. I think I wallowed in the trough of every malicious emotion I could summon, none being too malicious for the depth of my hurt.

Then before going to bed that night I did something I try to make a habit of doing. I just let go of all of those hurts, and I prayed for the lady who hurt me. Sleep came easily. I knew the weight of the emotional baggage I had collected during the day had gotten a whole lot lighter, even if it wasn't instantly gone. Sleep is my trusty barometer for such things, and I slept!

Now, when I spied that lady in the back of the church at my dad's wake, I realized just how light the load had actually become. A feeling of excitement came over me as I waited for her to inch her way up the aisle and finally reach me. I knew how *I* felt, but this was our first encounter since the ugly episode, and I had no idea how much heat lingered in her memory.

I soon found out. As she approached, we both knew we needed a hug. So we hugged! Then, without hesitating, she asked for forgiveness. At that moment I understood I had really forgiven her many months before, maybe as I prayed for her the day the event happened; maybe not. It didn't matter. There, standing beside my dad's casket, the case was closed. I knew my dad probably had another of his many prayers answered.

Why Forgive?

One of the best reasons I know to forgive is found in the Lord's Prayer: "forgive us our debts, as we forgive our debtors." While some may not agree, I think this means exactly what it says—that God forgives us as we forgive others. But what happens if we do not forgive? Jesus Himself gives the answer to that in Mark 11:26: "But if ye do not forgive, neither will your Father which is in heaven forgive your trespasses."

The apostle Peter once asked Jesus how many times he needed to forgive someone who had wronged him. "Seven?"

Not even close. Jesus said, "Seventy times seven!" In other words, as often as necessary.

Then Jesus added a little parable to His answer, about a king who wanted to settle his accounts with his servants. One of them owed him a huge sum of money and wasn't able to pay. When the king ordered that he and his family be sold to pay the debt, the servant pled for the king's patience and promised to pay it all.

The king was touched by this servant's sincerity, and instead of waiting patiently for the money, he forgave the whole debt.

One would think such a compassionate gesture would be recompensed by the servant passing on the kindness. But this pardoned servant had no such inclinations. Instead, he found a fellow servant who owed him a fraction of his own forgiven debt, grabbed him by the throat and proceeded to shake the living daylights out of him. Then he ushered him off to prison until he could pay.

When his fellow servants found out about the incident, they hurried off to their master and reported it. The errant servant was summoned, soundly chastised, and himself imprisoned until he could repay the now-reinstated debt.

It is important to remember that this is a parable, not a factual story. In any event, the unforgiving servant had learned nothing about forgiveness by being forgiven. Forgiving and being forgiven really are inseparable. If one does not learn that in the process of being forgiven, God may have to return His student to the classroom to learn it all over again.

Now this may sound selfish, but I can't think of a better reason to forgive someone than to ensure that God will, in turn, forgive me. Whether or not I feel like forgiving, I need to face the fact that to forgive and to be forgiven go hand in hand.

Forgiveness, however, goes far beyond pure selfishness. When Jesus was dying on the cross, in one of His final acts of compassion toward those who crucified Him, He prayed, "Father, forgive them; for they know not what they do" (Luke 23:34). One would have to twist that prayer completely out of shape to read anything like selfishness into it. In fact, forgiveness is the ultimate act of unselfishness.

Beyond Pardon

A number of years ago, the parents of a young student I was counseling called me, very distraught. A little while later they were sitting in my office telling a bizarre tale. Their son, apparently angered by some of their parental restraints on his personal freedoms, had decided to retaliate by placing a particularly noxious liquid at the base of his bedroom walls so it could slowly absorb up the wallboard, ruining the walls. By the time these parents discovered what their son had been doing, the walls were ruined and the only fix to the mess was completely gutting the room and starting over.

But they had not come to talk with me about fixing bedroom walls. They needed a fix for their son. They were so angry and hurt they were not at all sure they even *wanted* him fixed right away. What he really deserved was punishment, and they just couldn't think of one severe enough to fit the crime.

To complicate the picture, Christmas was rapidly approaching, and there was simply not enough money in the family budget to redo the bedroom and still put even modest gifts for everyone under the tree. In all fairness, the only one who really should suffer in this dilemma was the one who created it in the first place. This wayward son needed to learn a thing or two about the high cost of his crime. As we talked that day, we gradually realized that maybe the whole family needed to learn something about that cost. They left with a plan.

That evening, they called their three children

together in front of the fireplace for a talk. Needless to say, considerable anxiety hovered over this little summit as Mom and Dad prepared to deliver a verdict. Even the two children who were not guilty feared the price of their brother's crime. The little villain, however, was still bemoaning his limited freedom and didn't seem to care one way or the other. That added an uneasy element of disgust to this otherwise cozy setting!

The parents wasted no time getting to the point. Reviewing the facts was unnecessary, but they did anyway. That was part of the point. Every time someone breaks a rule, a debt is incurred, and someone needs to pay. In a gesture of love and compassion, they did not attach their son's name to this ledger. But guilt has a way of autographing the guilty, and a perfect stranger could have picked the guilty son out of this lineup.

In their next gesture of love and compassion, they announced their verdict on the bedroom dilemma. Christmas was near and this was no time to be settling scores. In a symbolic application of a typist's "White-Out," they simply forgave their son's errant behavior. That did not take care of the costly reconstruction project, but the parents had a plan for that, too. Since someone has to pay a price when someone errs, they decided to pay it all themselves and forgo any semblance of the usual Christmas they might have enjoyed with each other. They would do without gifts this year, but the bedroom would be redone. And there *would* be gifts under the tree for three precious children, along with a note to their wayward son on which was written, "Forgiven. Love, Mom and Dad."

Then they went on to explain that one time, a couple thousand years ago, there was a similar meeting at which scores needed to be settled and debts needed to be paid. One man was at that meeting who offered to pay everyone's debt; and it cost Him His life. The man's name was Jesus.

By now these three children sat there awed. They somehow knew they were looking into the face of that same Jesus, and He was called "parents." And these parents were looking into three precious hearts that Jesus had just touched. This family's story is still being written, but the ending had just changed.

Forgetting?...That's God's Job

Forgetfulness is often considered a malady of the aging process and rarely, if ever, viewed as an asset. Why then do we so often hear the phrase "forgive and forget?" There seems to be a marriage between these two words—like "love and marriage" and "horse and carriage—and "you can't have one without the other." Well, you can. In fact, there would be no such thing as forgiveness if the person who forgives were subsequently required to forget and act as if nothing had happened.

Richard J. Foster, in his book entitled *Prayer*, quotes Helmut Thielicke, a German pastor who survived the Third Reich, as saying, "One should never mention the words 'forgive' and 'forget' in the same breath." Many unspeakable atrocities were committed during the Third Reich, and we owe men like Thielicke a debt for ensuring that we never forget them or pretend they didn't happen. But Thielicke survived those awful years, partly because he forgave his debtors and can now, without malice or malevolence, recount their evil deeds for us all to remember.

The story is told of a nun who was paying a routine visit to heaven. Before one of her trips, a friend approached her and made this request: "When you see God this time, would you ask Him what is the greatest sin I have ever committed?" No problem. The nun agreed to fulfill the request and return with God's reply.

Several days later the nun was back. When asked for God's answer, she replied simply, "He said, 'I don't remember.'" That little parable is a colorized version of Psalm 103:12 which reads, "As far as the east is from the west, so far hath he removed our transgressions from us."

That, I think, is the divine definition of forgetting. I think it is also a reminder that forgetting is God's job. If you have any illusions about it being your job, try forgetting something—anything. Forgetting is not an act of one's will. It is not something about which one can make a conscious decision and then simply carry it out. It just happens. In fact, it often doesn't happen. Forgiveness does not require it, and God doesn't either.

A Very Personal Story

In 1960, I was a graduate student at Columbia University Teachers College. I had just come from a mime presentation by doctoral candidates who needed a break and a breather from their intense study schedule. The acting was quite extraordinary, and one particular "actor" caught my eye and plucked a string somewhere in the remote fibers of my heart. I left the performance clutching the memory of his face.

Later that day, I walked out of one building on campus into an atrium leading to Whittier Hall where I lived. Out walked that memorable actor as he exited a building directly across from me. We met, as if providentially, in the middle. I complimented him on his superb miming. And then, almost ceremonially, we walked an imaginary aisle together to Whittier Hall where he, incidentally, did not live. Thus began a romance befitting Camelot.

Every day all that year, we fanned the flame that began in mime. We grew only closer and became best friends. And if the ultimate test of trust and friendship is that you trust someone you love with your very best friends, we both passed it. When I would be away for a few days, he would care for my friends as if they were an extension of me. And we grew even closer.

The next logical step in that closeness was to lock it in for life. But just as the key was approaching the lock, I received a phone call from my dad. He and I had a very good relationship, but sometimes his views and my views were perfect strangers. What he said to me in that call could not have been stranger. He admonished me to end the relationship.

Now I have to tell you, my dad was one of the kindest men in the whole world. He was also a very wise and godly man. Maybe that is why I listened to him and ended the relationship. Maybe I did so just because he was my dad. It doesn't matter. What does matter is that my relationship with my dad changed after that call. I began constructing a wall of resentment around him and blamed him for a loss I knew he could never understand, nor was I willing to let him.

Resentment is not a static emotion. It grows, not like a flower, but like an ugly weed. For many years I fed and watered that weed. Until one evening I can distinctly remember, I knew I had to confront my dad about that deep hurt. I really do not remember how I began. I only remember how we ended. We put our arms around each other, forgave, and through tears, shared the first real "I love you" we had had in years. Again, our relationship changed, this time forever.

There is something very tenderizing about the whole sequence of hearts touching, hearts hurting, hearts forgiving, and hearts reconciling. Life without hearts to touch is like a meal without food to eat—sadly empty. But hearts that touch sooner or later will hurt each other. That is just the way hearts are made. And every hurt needs healing. That is what forgiveness does. It heals. Healed hearts are reconciled hearts, ready to touch again.

Forgiveness That Heals

The story is told of Leonardo da Vinci who, as he was painting *The Last Supper*, had a bitter argument with one of his contemporaries. In a fit of spite, da Vinci decided to use the image of this man as his model for the face of Judas. Then as da Vinci painted his way along the supper table he came to Jesus—but he was simply unable to paint Jesus' face to his satisfaction. After many tried and failed attempts, he realized that his feelings about his scorned contemporary were slowly changing and his anger toward him was almost gone. Had the face of Jesus really transformed his heart?

Apparently it had, because da Vinci then painted a loving Jesus using the same model he had used to paint a loathsome Judas. And if you look carefully at a painting of da Vinci's "Last Supper," you will note the striking resemblance in the faces of these two incongruous models. Da Vinci had discovered the practical healing power of forgiveness.

Better Late Than Not at All
But Oh! the Pricetag

Forgiveness has no risks, only rewards. Refusing to forgive or failing to ask for forgiveness has no rewards, only risks, not the least of which is regret.

I know. A student whom I had been counseling came to my office one day needing to make a phone call. He had no money for the pay phone so I offered him my office phone and then left him alone to afford him some privacy. After he had finished and I returned, I discovered that a Dictaphone I had in my briefcase was missing.

I confronted him, and he vehemently denied taking it. But there is something about guilt that wears on one like ill-fitting clothes. I reminded him of the seriousness of theft, particularly when the stolen item is a piece of state property, and that I would need to report this to the police. He seemed not to care, but I knew him well enough to know this was a facade. I also knew him well enough to know that once he had declared his position, a bolt of lightning was not likely to uproot it.

So I set out to teach him a lesson. I called the police. They interrogated him in my office, and I sat in on the interview at their request. I was sorry I did and even more sorry I had called them in the first place. Their wear-'em-down tactics had no limits, but they were no match for this boy's resolve. Within five minutes, I could see that this pursuit of the truth would be fruitless, but the police needed over two hours to become convinced.

By then, the interview was over, and the school busses were ready to leave for home. Nothing more was ever said about the Dictaphone. Our counseling sessions continued even as his theft record grew. While our relationship was somewhat strained, it was still one of the best he had. He was mostly lonely and a loner.

He finally graduated and went out into the world. I lost track of him. Then before long his name appeared in the paper as a newly fingerprinted tenant in a state prison. This time he was involved in a major theft and was serving an extended sentence. But true to his real character, once the hardened facades were cracked, he was a model prisoner and was granted early parole.

Just a few days later, he was tragically killed in an automobile accident. But that is not the end of that story.

On July 1, 1995, I retired from my role as school psychologist at the school where this boy had attended. The Dictaphone saga had long since found its way into a file of forgotten memories, or they had, until I heard about his death. Now, as I was emptying my desk of twenty-five years' worth of memorabilia, I reached to gather some final items from the last drawer, and an eerie piece of familiar metal touched my hand. There was that Dictaphone, neatly placed where it would not easily be found but still sufficiently returned to satisfy even the cruelest and most sensitive conscience.

I cannot describe the agony of that discovery. Flashing across my mind was the horrendous scene a few years earlier that occurred just on the other side of the desk where I was sitting. I could only wonder how differently this story might have ended had I, one of the few friends he ever had, just called him in, put my arm around him and assured him I was still his friend, told him if he took that Dictaphone, I forgave him, and asked for his forgiveness if he didn't. If only I had called on God for help that day instead of the police. If only. . . I'd have given a zillion Dictaphones in exchange for a different ending. The only ending I had now was regret. I have since added a resolve never again to walk away from a transgression unforgiven and always to work at designing a better plan for redemption than a potential prison term.

Forgive, Then Drop It

A couple weeks ago our pastor preached the last in a series of sermons on reconciliation. The series was timely, since many relationships among the congregation had been seriously marred. The message was inspiring, but it was the ceremony afterward that put a little lump in my throat.

As we entered the sanctuary that morning, we were each given a small white stone and instructed to hold it during the service. During the sermon we were encouraged to recall every hurt and anger and unforgiveness we could think of and symbolically place it on that stone. At the end of the service we were invited to walk to one of several designated wastebaskets in the sanctuary and get rid of the stone.

A solemn hush permeated the sanctuary as one by one the crowd made its way to a basket. The only perceptible sound was the thud of those stones dropping. As we completed this symbolic act of forgiveness, a pall of oppression lifted as surely as if a curtain were rising. And in another symbolic act, before returning to our pews, we each picked up the Communion elements and celebrated our reconciliation as we broke bread and drank wine together.

There is something very healing about forgiveness, but there is something even more rejuvenating about letting go of what you have forgiven. That whole series of sermons on reconciliation had been drawn together in this moving symbolic celebration of forgiving and letting go.

The Assignment

- If someone has hurt you and you wish to heal, apply a symbolic "White-Out" and clear the slate. Not a word needs to be spoken in this simple demonstration of forgiveness.

- If you have hurt someone and need forgiveness, there is no better time than now to go and ask for it.

Now go find yourself a stone, let it represent all the weights you have just unloaded as you forgave and were forgiven, then toss the stone where you will never be tempted to pick it up again.

12

NOW GO. . .

erefore, and teach all nations,
baptizing them in the name
of the Father, and of the Son,
and of the Holy Ghost:
Teaching them to observe all things
whatsoever I have commanded you.

MATTHEW 28:19-20

On October 17, 1989, at 5:04 P.M., the Loma Prieta earthquake struck central California. The quake lasted only fifteen seconds, but the toll in death and destruction was heavy. Over sixty people lost their lives; there were 3,757 reported injuries; more than twelve thousand were left homeless, and property damage costs exceeded ten billion dollars.

On State Highway 1 near Watsonville, a bridge collapsed. Minutes later a California highway patrolman was speeding along that highway on his way to offer assistance to victims of the quake. He was not aware, as he flew onto the bridge, that the support columns under it had shaken loose during the earthquake, and his road was about to end. The skid and scrape marks he left on the pavement attested to his valiant split-second attempts to make sure his life did not encounter the same fate.

Fortunately, miraculously, even though the road abruptly ended there, his life did not. But it could have. His last autograph might have been the marks he left on the pavement as he tried to avoid the crash. His last good-bye might have been the one he said to his family as he left for work that morning. His last meal might have been his lunch at noon. His last heroic deed might have been this wild ride that almost killed him. His last wish might have been that someone had warned him, stopped him, turned him around, done whatever was necessary to keep him from crashing.

Obviously no one knew about the collapsed

bridge. Any reasonable person, having known, would surely have taken immediate action—drastic action if necessary—to warn him that disaster lay ahead. There is some comfort in knowing that such a code of protection and altruism not only exists but is almost universally accepted and honored. Most of us, at one time or another in our lives, have benefited from someone who adhered to this code and warned us to slow down, detour, or make some other adjustment in our plans in order to avoid or survive a dangerous situation.

Don't Wait for a Warning!

A number of years ago while I was flying from Paris to New York, the pilot of our plane announced over the loudspeaker that we were experiencing some weather-related difficulty. I don't remember the exact bulletin, but I recall he was implicating "head-winds" as the culprit. We were instructed to keep our seat belts on unless it was absolutely necessary to move about the cabin. We followed his instructions.

The mild turbulence we felt at the time of the announcement quickly intensified. There was an ominous sense in the cabin that something more than headwinds was involved. Our flight was not just turbulent. I had been in turbulence before—severe turbulence—but this was different.

Before long our pilot was on the loudspeaker again. This time he announced that we were low on fuel and would be landing in Montreal, Canada, instead of JFK airport in New York as scheduled. With a sense of hushed fears, the passengers realized there were more pieces to this disturbing puzzle, and our pilot was presenting them on the installment plan. With several hundred miles of Atlantic Ocean yet to cross, we all doubted this aviation wonder could make it safely to *any* airport.

At transatlantic speeds we soon covered those last several hundred miles to Montreal. Before we had time to dwell on our dilemma, another announcement came over the loudspeaker. This time the pilot was telling us we were about to land. What followed was like a page out of Dante's *Inferno*.

During those final moments just before landing, when flight attendants are normally strapped into their jump seats, ours were passing through the aisles, methodically checking every passenger's seatbelt and personally giving each one an extra tug. At a point when the plane should have been slowing down and cruising smoothly to the runway, ours was bobbing spasmodically and slicing the warm Canadian air with a fury few of us had ever experienced in a landing. These skies were definitely not friendly.

Searching for some reassurance, I looked out the window. The runway below was lined with fire engines, ambulances, and emergency crews poised to give every scared one of us a whack at survival. But things didn't look very hopeful, and they felt even worse. I didn't need a pilot's license to know a plane couldn't land safely at the speed we were going. We seemed to have no brakes.

Then, just before touching down, our pilot zoomed us back up into those now even more unfriendly skies, and the whole terrifying ordeal started over. Except for that voice over the loudspeaker again, an eerie somber hush filled the cabin like a suffocating fog.

The announcement this time was a singular instruction, brief and to the point: "All passengers lower your heads." This time no flight attendants were on hand to make sure we obeyed; they were busy lowering their own heads. I distinctly remember the feeling of abandonment. It didn't feel good.

In any other setting, this solemn bowing crowd might have been mistaken for a prayer meeting. In fact, many passengers were praying, audibly, in many languages, stumbling out pleas to God without regard for eloquence or propriety. We all had at least two things in common: we were afraid we were going to die, and we all wanted to live.

We all shared one other thing—time, precious little time, but at moments like these, one doesn't quibble over quantity. However, an imminent appointment with almighty God can be a sobering—almost paralyzing—experience. My feelings during these unnerving moments reminded me of a commonly reported dream sequence where one is being chased by a raging carnivore but has no power to run and no voice to call for help. There may be precious seconds or minutes at one's disposal, but the clutter of crisis leaves little room for serious soul-searching.

Our abrupt return to the skies and a second attempt at landing gave us a few extra minutes to process the unthinkable—but prepare? We were in a battle for our lives, and the battlefield is no place to be searching for survival gear.

As things turned out, on the second try, our pilot miraculously brought our speed machine to a reluctant, screeching halt, and all our lives were spared. Things could have been different, however, and our fates might have been forever sealed on the Montreal tarmac that day.

Eternity Is Serious Business

Every day thousands of fates are sealed into an eternity of either heaven or hell. There is often no warning, no fanfare, and particularly no time to prepare. If we're on the road to heaven, having made that decisive journey to the cross, it really doesn't matter. We have already heeded someone's warning about the hell at the end of the road and turned around. The fanfare in heaven already began the moment we fell on our knees at the foot of the cross, conceded our place among lost sinners, and reached up to take possession of God's gift of eternal life. We already have our ticket to heaven in hand, written in Jesus' blood and absolutely free.

If we're still on the highway to hell, however,

nothing in the world could matter more. Everyone traveling *that* highway eventually ends up in a crash, a crash in which there are no survivors. There are no rescue crews, no ambulances, no emergency rooms. Everyone is a fatality; there are no exceptions.

And we're all traveling on that highway unless we've been stopped, warned, turned around, or otherwise redirected by someone who is honoring not merely a code, but a commission—the Great Commission.

The Task Is Simple: Go!

That Great Commission was proclaimed over two thousand years ago by Jesus and is recorded in Mark 16:15: "Go ye into all the world, and preach the gospel to every creature."

This is not just an assignment; it's a commission. When such an honor is bestowed on someone in the military, everyone involved celebrates. The Great Commission, on the other hand, doesn't lend itself to pomp and celebration. In fact, there is usually no commissioning ceremony, no conspicuous badge to wear, no certificate to display on the wall, no monetary increment in one's paycheck. This commission is a simple, humble, earthy command to share the gospel of Jesus Christ with our world.

The "World" Is Wherever You Are

For some of us, the world where we preach the gospel might be right in our own home or our neighborhood, our workplace, even in our church. For others, it may require taking off to other continents—to exotic hot-beds of sensual charm, or lonely, scary, forbidding jungles. It may mean leaving everyone and everything we know and love and going where everyone and everything is unfamiliar, maybe even unfriendly.

Wherever our world is, knowing someone around us is destined for hell should be compelling in itself. Being commissioned to share the good news that there is another way, another itinerary, another destination is a truly awesome, invigorating responsibility.

All Parties Benefit When the Gospel Is Shared

Every person on earth falls into one of two categories. Either we are in need of the gospel—or we should be sharing it with "all the world."

I recently heard about a nurse in England who regularly cared for a patient who was in a coma. There was little encouragement that the patient would recover, but that didn't deter this nurse. Every opportunity she got, she talked to her patient about Jesus and the gift of salvation He gave on the cross at Calvary. She had no confirmation that her comatose patient was getting the message. But she didn't need confirmation. She had a commission.

At the end of a long struggle to survive, the patient came out of her coma. Some of her first words were to her nurse: "Thank you for talking to me; I heard every word you said." By her own report, she entered her coma bound for an eternity in hell and came out of it redeemed for heaven.

Sharing the gospel is the most generous act of kindness one can possibly perform. It may not be a particularly popular kindness, and as with any gesture of generosity, it may even be rebuffed. It is important to note, however, that the Great Commission has no qualifiers. The command is simply to "go" and share the Gospel, whatever the response.

That of course is not a license for rude, in-your-face, like-it-or-lump-it arrogance. Most of us have, at one time or another, encountered that kind of misplaced, saintly enthusiasm, and we wish the good Lord would retire the saint.

But even though a messenger may be hopelessly flawed, the message is what matters. There is no retirement from the Great Commission. As long as we are living, that commission will be ours.

Now Go!

The story is told of a rancher in New Mexico who had three sons, Monte, Marvin, and Melvin. Monte was the middle son, Melvin was the eldest, and Marvin the youngest. Their majestic ranch sat on a high plateau in the plains of New Mexico and spread out thousands of acres from home base. To give you an idea of the magnitude of this estate, picture sixteen adjoining sections, each carefully measured into six hundred-acre plots. The place teemed with peace and prosperity.

This idyllic setting, however, was often interrupted by vicious snowstorms that moved in with little or no warning. The father, recognizing the gravity of these occasions, developed what he called "the Storm Plan." When a storm was forecast, the plan was activated, and everything else went on hold.

On one such occasion, they were given forty-eight-hour notice of an impending severe blizzard. Without hesitation, this father and his three sons spread out over their vast acreage to secure shelters and reassure cattle who seemed to have their own sense of foreboding. Forty-eight hours later, the storm was still only a prediction.

On the heels of the first warning came another, this time for a storm within twenty-four hours. Undeterred by a false alarm, they set out again with as much commitment to their Storm Plan as the first time around. When the next night arrived with no storm, they remained even more committed to their Storm Plan. It was a good plan; in fact, it was the only plan that could ensure a secure haven in any storm. They knew that sooner or later that storm would move in.

The next morning there was another bulletin indicating the storm would hit that night. Confident they had ample time to prepare for this one, Monte, Marvin, and Melvin got up, completed their morning chores, and were about to head off to school. Their father stopped them at the door. As he had looked out over the New Mexico sky that morning, he knew, as only a seasoned rancher can, that this time the warning was off target in the opposite direction.

"They say the storm will be here tonight, but I believe it will be here by noon today. I want each of you to go to your designated part of the ranch, secure it, and be back here by 9:00 A.M. Even if you can't secure it all, be back here by 9:00 anyway, and we will all go out together and secure your part." It was 7:00 A.M.

Off they went in four different directions. By 9:00 A.M., the storm had already hit. The father arrived at the designated rendezvous on time, as did Monte and Melvin. Marvin was not there. They waited until 9:15. Then the father led his two sons into the safety of the house and told them, "You boys are finished. I want you to stay here while I go out and find your brother."

He donned his hat and walked to the door. Just as

his hand reached the knob, he felt someone grasp his shoulder. He turned and saw the face of his middle son, Monte. With respectful determination, Monte told his dad, "Till everybody's home, nobody's finished."

With that, the three of them hopped into their four-wheel drive vehicle and started out to search for Marvin. As they reached his assigned area, the storm was at its peak. And there in a ditch off the side of the road, they saw Marvin's truck, turned on its side. There too was Marvin, shaken but unharmed. After relating the details of his accident, he said, "I stayed here because I knew you would be out to find me."

As the four of them headed home together to wait out the storm, the father couldn't get his mind off the words of his middle son, Monte: "Till everybody's home, nobody's finished."

Look Up: Storm Clouds Are Gathering!

Unless one has his proverbial head in the sand, one knows something catastrophic and unprecedented is about to happen. Storm clouds are gathering, on Wall Street, in the Middle East, in the unparalleled rash of severe storm systems worldwide, in the pit of more and more empty stomachs on the one hand and gluttonously full ones on the other, in the heavy hearts of weary men and women across the globe. From the pulpit to the newsroom, there is an unsettling sense that planet earth has slid off its axis and is about to self-destruct.

Admittedly, not all is gloom. Some optimists still put a weirdly positive spin on the most depraved of behaviors and ominous of events. There are always those who will endlessly defend the cup as half full when, in reality, it is not even half empty; it is hopelessly shattered.

The Gospel of Luke tells us in Chapter 21, verse 28, that "when these things begin to come to pass, then look up, and lift up your heads; for your redemption droweth nigh"—redemption, that is, for those who "believe on the Lord Jesus Christ and [are] saved" (Acts 16:31).

There is no other way to be redeemed, no other way to be saved, no other way to heaven, except by way of the cross. Every other way, no matter how noble or benevolent or upright, tragically leads, in the end, to a real, inescapable, everlasting hell. The gathering clouds are foreboding only to those who have not chosen the way of the cross, those who have not accepted God's Storm Plan.

Sadly, many are lost in the storm, sitting in the ditch, tipped on their side, who choose *not* to be rescued. Some don't believe the forecast, or they misjudge its ferocity. Others don't trust the rescuers or feel they have plenty of time to design their own rescue.

That, however, does not alter the Great Commission. Most people in need of the gospel are not clamoring to hear it. Most are unaware they are lost, and unlike Marvin in the ditch in New Mexico, they are not "dying" to be rescued. Still, the good news of salvation must be told, and God's messengers are commissioned to tell it.

Jesus Has Your Ticket, and the Cost to You Is Nothing

Steve and Annie Chapman sing a very moving and powerful song entitled, "I Dreamed I Searched heaven for You." They describe a heartbreaking futile search of every nook and cranny in heaven for a particular familiar beloved face. It isn't there. They ask the angels if they have seen that face. They haven't. Tragically, not everyone will be there. While heaven has plenty of room, and Jesus offers free tickets to all who ask, that search in heaven will turn up a long, sad list of absentees. We are all blessed with the freedom to choose what we will do with Jesus. We will all finally answer to Almighty God for the decision we make.

The Assignment

If you've already been to the cross, humbly accepted what you could not do for yourself and what only Jesus could do for you, and are on your way to an eternal home in heaven, go and share it with others. If not, right now is the only moment you are certain to have for turning around and heading home. Godspeed!

ABOUT THE AUTHOR

Martha Boshart is a retired school psychologist, having worked thirty years both in the public school system and with several agencies dealing with the developmentally disabled. She taught psychology at Kinnaird College for Women in Lahore, Pakistan, for one year. Prior to becoming a psychologist, she was a registered nurse. She is a graduate of House of the Good Samaritan School of Nursing, Watertown, New York, and Teachers College, Columbia University. She has traveled extensively throughout the world, and currently resides in Lowville, New York. She is a member of the First Church of the Nazarene in Watertown, New York.

Inspirational Library

Beautiful purse/pocket-size editions of Christian classics bound in flexible leatherette. These books make thoughtful gifts for everyone on your list, including yourself!

When I'm on My Knees   The highly popular collection of devotional thoughts on prayer, especially for women.
    Flexible Leatherette. $4.97

The Bible Promise Book   Over 1,000 promises from God's Word arranged by topic. What does God promise about matters like: Anger, Illness, Jealousy, Love, Money, Old Age, and Mercy? Find out in this book!
    Flexible Leatherette. $3.97

Daily Wisdom for Women   A daily devotional for women seeking biblical wisdom to apply to their lives. Scripture taken from the New American Standard Version of the Bible.
    Flexible Leatherette. $4.97

My Daily Prayer Journal   Each page is dated and features a Scripture verse and ample room for you to record your thoughts, prayers, and praises. One page for each day of the year.
    Flexible Leatherette. $4.97

Available wherever books are sold.
Or order from:

Barbour Publishing, Inc.
P.O. Box 719
Uhrichsville, OH 44683
http://www.barbourbooks.com

If you order by mail, add $2.00 to your order for shipping.
Prices are subject to change without notice.